A YEAR IN A ROCK GARDEN

An Organic Gardening Guide

By Ron Kushner

This book can be purchased through
http://www.ronsorganicgarden.com

Man – despite his artistic pretensions, his sophistication and his many accomplishments – owes his existence to a six inch layer of topsoil and the fact that it rains.

Author Unknown

PREFACE

I never planned to have a rock garden. I bought a half-acre property in 2006 and set about designing the garden almost immediately after signing the agreement of sale. The initial notes and sketches included a large potager (kitchen garden), a woodland garden, perennial beds, a tropical bed, dwarf fruit trees and a variety of shrubs and trees around the house. The main expense and commitment was a 16' long pergola as an entry way parallel to the house between the driveway and the front door. No rock garden.

The first year was an incredible flurry of activity. Compost bins constructed, a woodland garden created, 12' long raised beds installed for vegetables, perennial beds constructed and many, many plantings. On the west border of the property was a large berm, about 30' long and 10' wide with a large weeping cherry tree (*Prunus subhirtella* 'Pendula') on the north end which kept half of the berm in partial shade and the other half in full sun. It was raised about 3' at its highest point and contained a few partially buried rocks and was mainly weed covered. I cleaned out a section on the sunny end and planted some Phlox (*Phlox paniculata* 'David'), bee balm (*Monarda didyma* 'Coral Reef') and evening primrose (*Oenethera* 'Blushing Rosie') as a start to yet another perennial bed. Still, no rock garden.

In the fall of the second year with the majority of my gardens in fairly good shape, weeded and mulched, I decided to attack the weeds on the berm. Being a confirmed, hopelessly organic gardener it was hands and knees all the way with a soil knife and pruners. Wild strawberry, mugwort, encroaching crabgrass from the surrounding lawn, yellow nut sedge and all the other "usual suspects" were finally dug out and cleared off the surface of the berm. The soil seemed to be fairly decent – not quite the loam and humus I would have liked but certainly not the compacted clay that existed elsewhere around the property. I had the good fortune of access to a nearby farm's compost pile and covered the entire berm with 3" of shredded manure, garden debris and leaves for the winter. It was still my intention to design and plant a combination of perennials and annuals in the spring, as this "berm" was very visible from the house and our rear deck.

Like all gardeners, past and present, the joys of one's labor comes often at some point between the time the tools are put away in late afternoon (or not put away), cocktail hour or sundown with a stroll through the garden. It is a time to appreciate what has been accomplished, to plan the next priority or to simply enjoy the garden with its plants in place, or to come. It was one of these strolls, looking at the newly weeded and mulched "hunk" of real estate that simply screamed "rock garden". To me it was perfect. Sun, shade, good soil and a great place for a low-growing, xeric, colorful and interesting plant collection. It may have been my visits to many rock gardens, reading about them or experiencing them naturally in years past on mountain hikes but the decision was made. It will be a rock garden!

 The immediate problem was that my "berm" had only a few scattered rocks. I needed more. I read about the importance of "similar" rocks, mimicking those existing naturally, screes, etc., etc. and decided to simply accumulate rocks from wherever I could find them. Trips in my pick-up truck back and forth to work and whatever errands I had to complete in the course of my days took me over low bridges, streams, construction sites and dumping areas where rocks were readily available for the taking. I picked up one or two at a time, choosing those that looked interesting and that I could lift myself. Through the course of the winter I gathered these rocks and placed them here or there in proximity that (to me) looked rather natural and provided plenty of spaces for the plantings to come. By the time winter ended, the rocks were all in place, ready for spring planting.

 Selecting the initial plants for the new rock garden was a pleasureful project for that first winter. I poured over catalogs, guidebooks, rock garden bibliography, and magazines ending up with a list of about 300 "must have" plants. I measured the areas around the rocks, drew up a preliminary design and calculated that, at most, 40 plants could work.

 As the catalogs came over the course of the winter, I chose (arbitrarily, I admit) about 25 plants that appealed to me for one reason or another. Flower color, spread, foliage, winter interest with all supposedly hardy in my zone 6 garden. Through the next spring and summer I would fill in available spots with plants from local nurseries, catalogs, and friends, whatever.

This book represents a calendar year, the second since the garden was initially planted.

Figure 1 Berm after weeding and mulching before installation of rock garden.

ACKNOWLEDGMENTS

I would like to thank the owners of the rock gardens mentioned in this book for their generous time, conversation and valuable input.

Mostly I would like to thank my wife, Sheryl, for without her love and support, this work would not be possible.

CONTENTS

Preface

Acknowledgments

Chapter 1   January
Chapter 2   February
Chapter 3   March
Chapter 4   April
Chapter 5   May
Chapter 6   June
Chapter 7   July
Chapter 8   August
Chapter 9   September
Chapter 10 October
Chapter 11 November
Chapter 12 December

Plant Lists
Glossary
Bibliography
Sources
Index
Photograph Index
Biography

NOTE: Color versions of the images contained in this book can be found on Ron's website, www.ronsorganicgarden.com.

CHAPTER 1   JANUARY

On a cold January morning I visited the Brooklyn Botanic Garden in New York City to see their rock garden in the snow.

The garden first opened in 1917 and it is really some experience to see so many plants in such a natural setting. Many of the rocks installed originally are really huge boulders and in most rock gardens these immense rocks would be out of place and out of scale. In this particular setting they frame the garden beautifully along with a backdrop of woody shrubs and trees comprised of viburnums, maples, pines and spruces.

This rock garden is actually a combination of environments including an area for acid loving plants, dry tolerant plants, a pond for aquatic plants, a scree for dwarf alpine plants and a shade loving plant area .It would be very difficult for the average homeowner to try to establish an area to support all of this varied plant life without an immense portion of land. Most of us must settle on only a portion, depending upon our available land, location and contours.

Although snow covered and the paths icy, it was still easy to understand the overall design and to identify many plants both by foliage and labels. The larger azaleas and rhododendrons were clearly visible along with many dwarf conifers including yews, junipers, dwarf spruces and firs.

I was particularly interested in the plants that were growing over the lower rocks and peeking up through the snow. Lots of thyme was evident (such as Thymus x citriodorus) with green leaves clamoring over the rocks in clear view and covered with snow in some spots. Also Thymus herba-barona (caraway
thyme) with 18" stems loaded with seedpods protruding from the snow.

Sagina subulata (scotch moss) formed dense beds of moss-like green, tiny leaves covering the faces of buried rock. Phlox subulata (moss pink) was found here and there loaded with green leaves showing 6-8" *stems surrounded by snow. Mazus reptans 'Albus' also showing lots of low-matted green leaves in spots where the snow had melted. Dianthus gratianapolitanus also appeared here and there and I was especially happy to see their green, spiky leaves as this plant is also growing in my own garden.*

Some sedums were also showing their green leaves in the snow: Sedum cyaneum and S. reflexum (yellow stonecrop). Borders of larger rocks and boulders were covered with rock cotoneaster (Cotoneaster horizontalis) spreading everywhere with loads of persistent red berries looking lovely in the snow.
This cotoneaster, like some of the larger evergreens, would also not be a plant found in most rock gardens due to its size and spreading nature.

One of the reasons I love rock gardens so much is that in any season there is so much to see. Yes, many plants are not visible at all times but architectural interest created by the overall design, lay of the land, protruding rock surfaces and certain plants are always evident, interesting and delightful.

JANUARY

There is something special about a garden in winter dormancy; a kind of peace not present during the growing season. With the ground frozen and many plants either invisible or at least showing brown, dead stalks, it is amazing to see how much foliage is actually still visible. Looking closely, truly wonderful patterns of color and texture become apparent.

Dianthus gratianopolisitanus 'Firewitch' showing green foliage as if it were summer time, although not as abundant. *Artemisia versicolor* 'Seafoam' (curlicue sage) still showing blue-green foliage here and there contrasting nicely with the green stems of *Penstemon pinifolius* 'Nearly Red' (pineleaf beardtongue).

More green and spreading foliage includes *Teucrium aroanium* (gray creeping germander), *Iberis sempervirens* 'Little Gem' (dwarf candytuft) and *Thymus serpyllum* (creeping thyme).

Contrasting colors are also vibrant at this time of the year: the blood-red leaves of *Bergenia* 'Bressingham Ruby' (heartleaf), the beet-red and green foliage of *Penstemon* 'Mystica' and the maroon and green, whorled leaves on the *Euphorbia x martini* (Martin's spurge).

Still other plants here and there showing green foliage include: *Penstemon x mexicale* 'Red Rocks', *Saponaria ocymoides* (Cote d'Azur pinks), *Armeria maritima* 'Pink Lusitanica' (sea-thrift), *Sedum dasphyllum* 'Major' (stone crop), *Anthemis tinctoria* 'Susanna Mitchell' (Marguerite daisy), *Arctostaphylos coloradensis* (hybrid manzanita), *Digitalis obscura* (narrow leaf foxglove), *Penstemon* 'Blue Midnight', *Achillea* 'Moonshine' (moonshine yarrow), *Origanum* 'Rotkugel' (ornamental oregano) and *Pelargonium endlicherianum* (Turkish geranium).

The *Pelargonium* is a surprise to me, as I never considered the genus as a whole hardy in my Zone 6. This plant never grew very well the first year but it developed slowly and increased its foliage at a steady pace. Even though frozen now, its leaves are holding their shape and fullness.

Of pleasing contrast, also showing colorful foliage, is the *Picea abies* 'Little Gem', along with the gray-green spikes of the *Lavandula angustifolia* 'Nana' (dwarf English lavender), the brown-maroon clusters of *Sempervivum* (hens and chicks) and the gray-green foliage of the *Hymenoxys*.

Should rocks be required for a rock garden at this time, one can always go to a local quarry or stone yard and buy whatever stone may be required. This is the most expedient way if the sizes, coloring, shapes, etc. are to your liking. If you only need a few, here and there, January is a good time to look for rocks locally. Herbaceous vegetation has mostly died back and rocks are more visible. Obviously, private residential or commercial property must be avoided unless the owner is contacted.

Many roadside areas and overgrown woods may contain a rock or two, usually along with trash, which somehow accumulates in these spots. Keep your eyes open as you drive around.

Also, many construction projects could either be underway, completed or halted due to cold weather, which could involve various types of stonework. Many times I have been given left over stone by contractors not wanting to haul it away.
Most Townships and municipalities have dumps or transfer stations that provide recycled materials for free. Again, I have found many suitable stones in this manner.

The matching of stone, "geological correctness" or coloring did not seem to be important to me in my own garden. Interesting shapes and a pleasing placement seemed most important. Ultimately, plants will grow and creep around and over the stones so that only portions will be visible. The stone mulch I use further connects the entire collection and creates a coordinated picture.

The lack of foliage is an added benefit to placing rocks at this time of the year. They can be placed, viewed in various light, relocated and adjusted as needed in a most leisurely way. The time for new plantings and spring growth is a long way off. Once the ground can be worked and the rocks are in their correct position, it is important to bury them at least by one third to assure their permanence and to assure they don't move when stood upon.

January is the month to find last year's notes on the plants you wanted in your rock garden, re-read any magazine articles saved about rock gardens and start to plan what is to be ordered and planted in the coming spring.

Catalogs are an excellent source and the Internet is invaluable. The catalogs I use are listed in "Sources" in the appendix but there are many, many companies nationwide where appropriate rock garden plants can be ordered. Always check the description and the cultural requirements carefully, especially zone, light requirements and sizes (ultimate height and width). Color and bloom time are also important considerations along with rate of spread.

It is helpful to make a small drawing, to scale if possible and sketch in the location of those plants to be ordered. Be careful not to plan for planting too closely. Space needs to be available for air circulation, normal plant spread and mulching.

Plants can be purchased in basically two ways: "bare root" or "potted". I prefer not to buy bare root plants for my rock garden, even though this practice of shipping plants is becoming more and more popular. I always look for a plant that is to be shipped in a pot, regardless of how small the container.

When a potted plant arrives in the spring, it can be unpacked and left in the pot to harden off and to put out new growth for a very long time prior to planting. Of course, attention must be paid to assure it receives adequate light and moisture. The plant can be seen immediately and when planted can be marked, labeled, mulched and is constantly in sight. Its progress can be monitored from day one.

Bare root plants come in plastic or are wrapped in damp newspaper, shred or whatever, need the proper amount of moisture (who knows what that is?) and once planted beneath the surface are out of sight (and out of mind?). Of course the spot can be marked and labeled but one never really knows when the plant stem will break the surface, in some cases, not until the second season. Mulch becomes a problem or at least, a question. Do you cover the area or leave it open? Will weeds pop up prior to the stem? Could the stem be mistaken for a weed? No, it's a pot for me!

NOTE: Many gardeners feel that a new potted plant, received from some distant nursery would fare better if it were removed from its pot, the original soil mixture shaken off and replanted into a pot with a closer soil mixture to their own garden soil. Its chance of survival would be, theoretically, much better.

This sounds like good advice but I've never had the time or patience to deal with a new plant in this manner. I allow my newly arrived plants to remain in their pots for a few days, watering as needed and allowing them to overcome the shock of the shipping experience. Generally, they remain on my deck under an awning to be safe from wind, direct sun and down pouring rain.

Once these few days have passed, it's into their new home, watered and mulched with stone. Out of approximately forty new plants and seedlings, I've lost only three. All of the plants ordered from a reputable nursery normally come with a guarantee for the first year. The nurseries listed in "Sources" in the appendix will re-mail a plant at no charge, no questions asked, if it doesn't survive. This is true even though it may be the fault of the gardener and not the plant itself.

This is a good time when shopping for plants to consider "native plants" vs. "alien plants". The definition of "native" has been manipulated and used throughout the country in so many different ways that the distinction is rather cloudy and confusing. Are they native to somewhere in North America? Are they native to a particular area within the country? If native to a certain state do they exist only at certain elevations, in bogs, etc.? For my purpose, native plants are those that have not been introduced from Europe, Asia or other areas but have been growing in a particular, local area since before the settlement of this country, including Native Americans. This definition may seem a bit strict but it is interesting to note that Native Americans moved plants around the country quite a bit!

Of course, when dealing with rock gardens, many suitable plants will be from environments rather foreign to your particular area, consequently "non-native". Nevertheless, it would pay to do some research as to what plants are native to your specific garden area. In many cases, the list is longer than one would expect. A good beginning source for native plants would be the local county extension agent (see "County State Extension Services" in Sources).

In my garden, many of the plants were chosen for their growth habit, interesting foliage and flowering habit and they are not native but well adapted. I felt that they provided plant diversity, nectar and color for attracting insects, hummingbirds and the like and hopefully an environment that a diversity of life, however minute, will flourish in.

This consideration of Native vs. Non-native is not only due to the plants and their growth; it has to do with the entire ecosystem that utilizes local wildlife for these plants, either for food, as a host for beneficial insects to lay their eggs or their ability to attract other beneficial insects, birds, mammals, etc.

One word of advice: Start your plant list this month but wait until February to actually order. Sit on your potential plant list for at least a month as the catalogs keep arriving right up until spring. You just may want to switch some "early decision" plants for a later "must have".

Should you be a beginning rock gardener or simply planning a future rock garden, this would be a good time to review the plant lists in the appendix, especially the list of plants that should never be planted in a rock garden.

Since this work is about rock gardens, some discussion is warranted regarding the terms used frequently to describe rock garden plants. The term "alpine" plant refers to a plant that grows naturally in an actual mountain setting and was originally named for the Alps in Europe. A "rock" plant or "rock garden plant" is one that may include alpine plants, but would also include any plant of the proper size and characteristics making it suitable for planting in a rock garden.

I suppose it is possible to specialize in plants from a certain region or to collect some particular family or genus of plants in a rock garden. It should be noted that in my garden I am looking for plants that appeal to me and that their arrangement, location and characteristics follow no specific guidelines whatsoever other than my own "whim".

Figure 2 Rock garden in January.

Figure 3 Euphorbia x martini in January.

Figure 4 Penstemon 'Red Rocks' in January.

Figure 5 Penstemon "Mystica" in January.

Figure 6 Lavandula Augustifolia 'Nana' in January.

Figure 7 Boulders at Brooklyn Botanic Garden in January.

Figure 8 Rock Garden at Brooklyn Botanic Garden in January.

CHAPTER 2 FEBRUARY

One of my favorite rock gardens to visit is at the New York Botanical Garden in the Bronx in New York City. On a chilly but sunny morning in February I took the train from Grand Central Station to see what the garden looked like in winter.

They charge an additional fee to enter the rock garden and some other attractions, which I gladly paid. After a pleasant walk through the arboretum I made my way to the rock garden. Much to my frustration it was closed for the winter season!

Surrounded by an 8-foot high cyclone fence and a padlocked gate my disappointment prompted me toward an idea: I'm already here, it's a beautiful day, why not hike around the perimeter of the entire garden? Perhaps I would get some nice views of the interior through the fence or even possibly a clandestine entry should the fence have a break somewhere.

A pleasant walk turned into an arduous hike through thick underbrush, felled trees and much foliage obscuring any hope of viewing plants inside of the fence (which remained perfectly maintained all the way around). Vines and briars continually snagged me and I tripped on more than one occasion, eventually ripping a leg of my trousers from the calf down. Finally, I made it back to the gate and my original point of departure more than an hour earlier.

The high point of that rock garden visit turned out to be my lunch at the Oyster Bar back at Grand Central Station and the iced-cold Sauvignon Blanc.

FEBRUARY

At the start of February my rock garden was totally snow-covered and now, in the first week, the temperature has climbed to 50 degrees leaving only patches of snow here and there. Most of the plants with visible foliage are flattened on top of their stone mulch and looking rather "beat up" from the last two months of ice, snow and frigid temperatures. The sun is warm and I'm yearning to start clipping brown stems and removing growth that appears dead but I know better.

It is still too early for any spring-cleaning and the ground is thoroughly soaked and still frozen in spots. A winter storm has been forecasted and at this time in mid-winter it pays to be patient. Even though many plants have brown foliage showing, there are still many green leaves so it is best to wait without doing more harm than good.

The lavender needs trimming, along with the *Gaura* and *Campanula*. Also, the long, brown daisy stems of *Hymenoxys acaulis*, *Penstemon* 'Blue Midnight', *Agastache* and Japanese blood grass (*Imperata*) all need to be clipped back prior to new spring growth. The garden has some leaf litter and small, fallen tree stems strewn about, all which must be left alone at this time. It would not be a good idea to be clamoring over the wet, partially frozen garden at this time. Time to go indoors for a nice cup of tea!

As I type these notes, snow has been falling as predicted all afternoon, through the night and into the morning, leaving a deposit of five inches so far. The rock garden has disappeared again, beneath a huge white mound, with only a few stems poking up through the snow. The snow is actually the best thing for the plants below, providing a natural mulch against freezing and thawing and ultimately a steady, "slow drip" of moisture once the winter draws to a close.

This is the month to release your order for plants for spring. Make sure that you have room for every plant and at least a rough idea of where each one will be planted. Don't assume that you will be able to simply "fit them in some place" as you will most likely be wrong. Also, as the season progresses, do not buy, order or accept any plant unless you have the spot already selected and ready to plant the new acquisition. This rule will take some discipline at first but will pay off through the years with a neater garden and a tremendous reduction of stress.

Even though the plant order is complete, this is also the time to establish a notebook of some sort for the coming year for additional plants to order (a "wish list", if you will). Plants that you see in other gardens, magazine articles, catalogs, etc. are all candidates for new plants. In my early gardening days I used to keep catalogs, magazines and notes in a big pile or box. It never worked. A simple list is easy to keep and can be referred to throughout the season whenever new plants are discovered or contemplated.

The most extensively used tool throughout the season in my rock garden is a soil knife (see "AM Leonard" in the appendix under "Sources"). It is used mainly for weeding, as it penetrates soil, stone mulch and just about anything in its subterranean path effortlessly. Also, it can be maneuvered very close to existing plants without damaging their root systems. Generally, all that needs to be done is to sink the blade in close proximity to the weed, rock the handle once, gently and the weed usually pulls right out. A great expanse of garden area can be covered in this manner in a short period of time.

This soil knife is also useful for cutting any thicker existing roots that may be in the way of new planting areas. One edge of the blade is serrated, which works sort of like a mini- saw blade.

When planting or transplanting, the knife is very helpful for loosening up soil at the new location. I don't think it is a candidate for replacing the traditional garden trowel but in many cases will do just as well. I still use my trowel for many tasks but the tiniest transplant or cutting.

Since most rock garden plants are normally small, a spade is rarely needed.

If you do not own a soil test-plugging tool, the knife can be used to obtain soil samples by cutting out a plug just below the existing soil or turf surface.

Plants can be divided using the soil knife and during the warmer months can even be used to clean up garden edges while weeding. It won't take the place of an edger but in a pinch does just fine.

Another tool that I use continually is a "pick mattock" especially made for gardeners (see "AM Leonard Co." or "Lee Valley Tools" in Sources). The "mattock" end is wider and chops out a larger amount of soil where the "pick" end is pointed and chops up soil easily. The handle is usually a foot or so long for comfortable leverage. It makes whatever depth or width hole is desired and is far more efficient and faster than any other means. Of course, for the tiniest seedlings my favorite tool is the soil knife.

The pick mattock is also excellent for weeding a large area in a very short period of time. It is especially useful for weeding an area that has not yet been planted. Each "stab" of the pick end not only brings up the roots of the weed, but also turns the soil slightly to ready the area for new planting.

Today it is nearing the end of February on a sunny but chilly Sunday afternoon. Winter snows have again melted, exposing my rock garden still in winter dormancy. I look at each plant, searching for a sign of spring. Alas, only one plant actually shows promise: The *Saxifraga arendsii* 'Purple Robe'. Most of the plant looks like the others except for six or eight bright green leaves amongst the seemingly dead foliage. The tiny leaves look similar to parsley and unmistakably showing the signs I am looking for. This plant is on the west side of the rock garden with the setting sun in its face. There is more cold weather to come before spring and still no work to be done at this time in the garden; but how nice to see those tiny leaves from a plant obviously more patient than its curator.

Figure 9 Rock Garden in Early February.

Figure 10 Rock Garden in February.

CHAPTER 3 MARCH

Near the end of March I visited the rock garden at Penn State College of Agricultural Sciences Cooperative Extension in Montgomery County, Pennsylvania. The garden is mulched entirely with a fine material resembling tiny pebbles known as "Turface" in the form of a scree (See Chapter 5 – May for a full description). It is situated in full sun on a relatively flat surface near the south end of a water feature. It is a small rock garden, roughly 15 feet in diameter but still contains a sizable amount of small plants.

Many of the plants were still dormant with lots of brown, untrimmed leaves and stems. An example being Carex 'Frosted Curls' and some other Carex species. Here and there were some Sempervivum tectorum (hens and chicks) unlabeled but showing bright, varying shades of maroon clusters.

The Penstemon pinifolius had fresh, green, upright growth, not with sprawling stems like those in my own rock garden. The following plants were showing fresh, new spring growth: Armeria maritima, Herniara glabra and Festuca glauca 'Elijah Blue'. A Hemerocallis 'Siloam Baby Talk' had much fresh "Iris-like" foliage pushing up out of the gravel mulch. A Sedum spurium 'Red Carpet' had many clusters of fresh, maroon-colored growth.

This rock garden had a label system comprised of vertical labels with no horizontal counterpart such as the ones I use (and recommend). The vertical piece was stuck into the ground with the label information written from top to bottom. They take up less room but they are annoying to read. You have to tilt your head at an uncomfortable angle to make out each name.

One of the plants, Opuntia spp. (Cholla) looked healthy and interesting and to me, very out of place in this northeastern rock garden. It was about 8" tall, loaded with spines and vertical, looking very "desert-like" and southwestern. Although I believe the selection of plants is the prerogative of the gardener, a rock garden does need some degree of "eco-logic". Rock and alpine plants, for example, in a northeastern United States garden surrounded by a dwarf banana would probably be just as unacceptable to me.

MARCH

March has finally arrived, along with steady snow, a winter storm watch and temperatures well below freezing. It is hard to believe that daylight savings time begins in one week and in two weeks I would normally plant my peas and early spring greens.

The rock garden is again snow covered and continuing its dormancy. Perhaps with the next thaw and moisture from the melting snow some spring growth will start to show and the gardening season will actually begin!

Once the snow is gone, March is a good time to have your garden soil tested if you have not already done so. Based upon the test results, any soil amendments required can be added prior to the actual planting of new plants. At the very least, you should know your soil pH (the measure of acidity or alkalinity of the soil). It is also helpful to know whether any major elements are lacking.

Garden centers and catalogs sell a variety of soil test kits. One of the simplest ways to test your soil is through your County Extension Service in the state where you are located. It will generally cost about $10.00 and once mailed to the proper testing agency the results are returned in about two weeks. Most garden centers will carry the proper mailing envelope complete with soil bag and instructions (see "County State Extension Services" in Sources).

Rock garden plants will adapt to a variety of pH levels but your soil should be in the vicinity of 6.6 to 7.0, as this range will accommodate a wide range of available plants.

Prior to submitting your soil samples, generally to a Land Grant State University, you will be directed to fill out a form listing the category of what you intend to grow. It is this information that the testing will respond to and any recommended requirements will be listed. You can then purchase any required amendments and apply them prior to actual planting time. I would strongly urge anyone to not purchase any product, regardless of what the label promises, until a soil test has been completed. In the early days of this country's agricultural history, it is said that a farmer could taste the soil and tell exactly whether the pH was high or low and what needed to be added. These days, I still believe a soil test is the best way to go (not to mention avoiding some parasitic disease).

Rock garden soil should be well drained with good aeration, containing some organic matter but not very rich. The garden being somewhat raised on a slope or berm, such as mine, provides for the best drainage. Some crushed stone or coarse sand mixed in wouldn't hurt.

The most important aspect of the soil, along with good drainage, is the organic matter. The rock garden doesn't need much due to most alpine plants doing fine in a non-rich medium. Most rock gardens are created some distance from any naturally occurring alpine setting and there must be enough to encourage the growth of bacteria and fungi, not to mention the rest of the "cast of characters" living in the soil and whose life style provides the nutrients in the form the plants can absorb.

The plants, in turn, secrete the nutrients through their roots that those millions of organisms devour to keep the growing cycle alive and healthy.

Many of these organisms, especially bacteria, fungi, one celled organisms and nematodes are killed by the addition of synthetic fertilizers, totally upsetting the healthy balance of life in the soil.

March could be the month that fertilizer is utilized as in many cases the end of the month turns warm and the soil can be worked efficiently.

My fertilizer schedule is composed of the following:

A. A shovel full of compost mixed well with the existing soil when a new plant is either planted or transplanted.
B. A mulch of well shredded leaves in the fall on any areas in between plants and not mulched with stone.
C. A thorough watering with a fish emulsion mixture when fresh, new green growth emerges in spring. The fish fertilizer is also used on new plants or transplants throughout the growing season whenever initial new growth is noticed.
D. Watering around the base of the plants and foliar feeding with a high quality compost tea monthly, throughout the growing season.

I do not recommend any high nitrogen fertilizer. The plants absorb the nitrogen and become especially attractive to insects such as aphids and leafhoppers. Also, plants high in nitrogen are often more susceptible to virus infection (see "Thresh, J.M." in bibliography).

When working on rock garden soil, a "perfect" soil composition is also not recommended. Unlike perennial beds and shrub beds, the rock garden soil should allow its plants to "struggle" a bit. In soil that is "just so", the most aggressive plant will normally flourish and start taking over, requiring an excessive amount of vigilance and maintenance.

As the warmer weather approaches, so does the gardener's need to be working in the soil. Starting too early is really a mistake. The soil could still be saturated and it is easily compacted at this time. If it is turned over it could easily be baked into large "bricks" that are tough to break up later. To tell if the soil is ready to be worked simply pick up a handful and squeeze it into a ball. Poke it with your fingers or drop it to the ground from a height of three to four feet. If it shatters, it's ready to be worked. If it keeps its shape or breaks only in half or in large "clumps" it is still too early. It needs to dry out more. The courser the soil (closer to sand) the more moisture it can hold and still be worked. The finer the particles (like clay) the less moisture it needs to be workable.

As I see the green to red tips of bulbs sticking up in areas other than my rock garden, I am sorry I did not plant some tiny bulbs in the rock garden last fall. They would be a most welcome sight at this time with the snow melting but most of the plants still in their dormancy awaiting the soil and air to reach warmer temperatures.

I must make a note to order some *Galanthus* (snowdrops), *Scilla*, and *crocus* bulbs to plant this coming fall.

It is now past the middle of March, a sunny, spring-like day with the temperature 63 degrees F. Time to start spring-cleaning in the rock garden. The first job is to remove any fallen debris, sticks, spent stems (past "winter interest"), fallen leaves and any blown in bits of trash. This is also the time to check each plant to insure it has not heaved out of the ground leaving some roots exposed. If this is the case, simply re-bury the roots and firm the soil around the plant.

As I work through the garden, using my soil knife I remove any weeds showing. At this time there is some wild strawberry, tufts of grass, mugwort and some chickweed. They are all easily removed and placed in my "compost" pail.

The *Aquilegia x caerulea* 'Red Hobbit' is showing a nice cluster of blue-green crinkled leaves. I carefully clip away all of the straw-like dead stems with a short-shaft pair of scissors; the kind with big handles and short blades (mine are actually for pruning bonsai plants and work well). It is important to be especially careful not to accidentally sever any of the tender, small young leaves.

Penstemon 'Red Rocks' has upright brown stems with many small, dead leaves. Lower down the stems become a very evident green with fresh green leaves. I clip off all the dead growth above until I hit the green of the stems, shortening the plant to a clump about 6" tall and 6" in diameter.

The *Saxifraga* (rock foil) has heaved a bit but is showing nice fresh green leaves. I settle it back into the ground carefully, but firmly. Some plants are looking really dead now with brown leaves and stems prostrate on their stone mulch. *Penstemon* 'Mystica', *Ceratostigma plumbaginoides* and *Geranium sanguineum* are three examples. These plants are best left alone at this early time. Hopefully, as the ground warms up and spring rains come, fresh growth will appear.

The *Sedum sieboldii* has a few long, dead stems with dried seed heads at the ends. These are snipped off all the way to the new, pale green leaf clusters forming at the base. They remind me of tiny artichokes.

Armeria maritima gets a haircut all around its perimeter and top growth trimmed until most of the brown, grass-like leaves are gone and only new green growth is showing.

Arctostaphylos x coloradoensis looks healthy with long stems trailing across the stone mulch with lots of green leaves showing.

The *Anthemis tinctoria* has fresh green leaves showing and lots of dead, brown stems and leaves, which are clipped off carefully (as one would "clean up" a houseplant).

Dead brown stalks of *Imperata cylindrical rubia* are cut down to the ground, even though no fresh growth is showing yet.

All the dead stalks of *Agastache* 'Acapulco Salmon and Pink' are cut down to about 2" above the crown with no new growth showing. The plant looks dead.

Penstemon has also all of its dead stalks cut to the ground and deep within the crown a few tiny, green leaves are visible.

The *Achillea x* 'Moonshine' has many nice green, fern-like leaves showing and only needs a few dead stalks clipped.
Verbena peruviana 'Red Devil' looks totally dead with prostrate gray branches lying all around. I knew it was doubtful that this Zone 7 plant would make it through the winter in my Zone 6 garden. I'll leave it alone for the time being. Its bright "electric" red blossoms were

certainly enjoyed all last summer. Perhaps I should have mulched it under straw for the winter? It is still early; perhaps I'll be surprised.

Asclepias tuberosa is showing fresh leaves at the crown with no trimming required.

Hymenoxys acaulis has its dead stalks cut to the ground with no new growth showing. The *Hymenoxys scaposa* is a small, round mound of thin green leaves requiring no trimming at this time.

Guara lindheimeri is a mass of brown stems and leaves, all of which are cut down to the ground.

Dianthus gratianopolitanis is showing a small mound of green leaves with only a few dead stems needing to be snipped off.

Lavandula angustifolia needs only its long, thin spike ends cut down to where the leaves are showing. The plant looks marvelous!

Campanula rotundifolia has all of its grass-like dead stalks cut off to about one inch above the soil line. Lots of fresh, new green leaves are showing deep in the crown.

Aconitum 'Blue Lagoon' has many new green leaves and requires no work at this time.

I trimmed only the long tips of the *Caryopteris x clandonensis* 'Longwood Blue' back to a strong pair of leaves. It's already looking too large for the rock garden and may have to be relocated. I'll give it this season before I decide for sure. This plant is supposedly a low growing, drought tolerant species. The foliage is soft, gray-green that deer tend to avoid. Clear blue flowers appear throughout late summer and early fall. With a light shearing, blossoming can be extended through the fall. After the plant is well established, an annual winter pruning back to about a foot or so will promote a nice, compact habit.

The entire rock garden needs fresh stone mulch but it is a mistake to reapply the mulch at this early date. The ground needs to warm up considerably and additional mulch would keep the soil cool. Once the night temperatures remain around 50 degrees F. new mulch can be applied.

Toward the end of the month I bought and planted two creeping phlox plants in the rock garden. Both were *Phlox subulata*, one 'Blue Emerald' and the other 'Fort Hill'. They were outside at Lowe's Garden Center and I was touched by their delicate, pale blue and dark pink blossoms at this early date.

I dug the holes with my pick mattock as the plants were in quart containers. I planted them with a bit of compost and watered them well. Their spring flowers are most welcome at this time. I wonder if they will be the first plants to bloom next spring.

Early the next morning I awoke to a 35 degree temperature with snow falling steadily.

March ended with a sunny day and no notable change in the rock garden. It looks clean and neat, the only blooming plants are the two *Phlox* recently planted. The *Forsythia* shrubs are starting to bloom and rain is forecast.

Figure 11 The rock garden at Penn State in March.

Figure 12 Close up view of Penn State's rock garden in March.

Figure 13 Rock garden in March after "Spring Cleaning".

Figure 14 Freshly planted Phlox subulata 'Blue Emerald' in March.

CHAPTER 4 APRIL

Susan Dana calls herself an "eclectic gardener". Her rock garden in Skippack, Pennsylvania was originally a run-off area to a retention basin 18 years ago. She never planted a tree nor added any rocks. As the rock garden was developed, she moved some of the rocks around for convenience of planting or aesthetics and let some of the tree "volunteers" take root and remain. What was originally all grass on a rock-strewn slope has become a lovely, natural, rock garden setting, made up almost entirely of wild plants. A small pond and a waterfall were added, which is now surrounded by small Juniper trees and Forsythia permitted to remain. Throughout the garden is Jewelweed (Impatiens pallida), along with Lilies, Black-eyed Susan and wild mint. There are violets all over, Lambs ear (Stachys byzantina) and Iris donated by a friend. Near the base of the rocks are some Peonies and Hibiscus with Primrose blooming all around, along with daffodils and a yellow-blooming Celandine (wood poppy) that I couldn't positively identify.

Susan's philosophy is that she wants the garden to be "informal and wild" without the look of any formal, "proper" maintenance or planting. This has certainly been accomplished and the lack of any labeling system helps her to keep the "look" that she desires. She does work very hard at the maintenance however, weeding (especially garlic chives) and keeping her "wild plants" in check.

After a summer rainstorm, she especially likes to sit on one of the larger stones near the water cascading down the rock-strewn garden grade simply enjoying the setting. I can't think of a better way to appreciate a rock garden.

APRIL

The first week of April has passed with rain almost every day. The sun is warmer and the afternoons are mild but still some early morning frost. The Oregano (*Origanum x rotkugel*) has green leaves showing here and there and last year's dead brown stems can now be cut away. The *Pelargonium* is showing lots of fresh, green new growth, along with the *Aconitum, Aquilegia, Geranium, Anthemis* and *Penstemon*.

The *Saponaria* is "greening up" nicely but no sign of flowering. The Japanese blood grass (*Imperata cylindrical*) is showing green and white shoots about an inch long coming up through the old brown sheaths. You have to look pretty closely to see them. Also, the *Gaura* has new red leaves throughout its crown.

Weeds are starting to sprout in the un-mulched areas and these will be teased out continually throughout the summer. Although it is a sunny afternoon, rain is again forecasted for tomorrow and through the weekend. There is no need for any watering at this time.

April is generally the month to begin planting throughout most of the United States. The extreme Northern and Southern Zones would be an exception, of course. As new plants arrive, place the pots in a sheltered spot for at least one to three days before planting. Shipping, transporting and varying temperatures are all shocking to plants. This time before actual planting is also a help if weather or your personal time constraints do not allow for immediate planting. If you have started seeds in pots, inside, these too should be held in a sheltered spot, outside for a few days (a process known as "hardening off"). Don't place your plants in full sun; a shady, bright spot is best.

Make sure you label everything. It is difficult to identify many plants at this early stage without mature foliage or flowers. Remember to be especially attentive to your watering. Even so-called "xeric" plants need water when planted and throughout their first year until they are mature with a well developed root system.

If possible, hold off on edging your rock garden until the summer months approach. During the edging process, annual weed seeds are brought to the surface in exposed, fresh soil and germinate in the moist weather of early spring.

Sculpture, in general, can serve an extremely beneficial purpose in bringing a garden design together. For rock gardens, care must be taken due to the smaller scale of the plants tucked in here and there or spreading around the various rocks and stones comprising the garden.

In larger garden areas from traditional perennial beds to large, public parks the artwork, in my opinion, is usually overdone. In many cases, the particular sculpture overshadows the surrounding area and creates more of an intrusion to the landscape than a supportive addition. Perhaps this phenomenon would be welcome in an outdoor art gallery or located on the grounds surrounding a building housing a famous collection.
Of course, the ultimate decision rests with the owner of any garden and his or her taste will prevail. Should they be a "patron of the arts" of some sort, anything could be installed from a huge hunk of welded steel (usually painted some garish color) in the name of "Modern Art" to a pile of terra cotta bricks resembling some sort of cairn.

In between, one could find anything from wind driven whirly-gigs to the recently popular placement of three round balls somewhere on their turf grass. In the older days of formal, European gardens it was sculpture of people, usually fighting, mostly naked or at least taking off their clothes.

In my own rock garden, I did want some sort of artwork, mainly to lend a touch of the human element to what I was doing; in some way, to create a personal touch to show that I was "in charge" rather than pretending that the environment and nature were solely responsible for its creation. Perhaps this is why people get tattooed?

After searching for a year, I found what I considered suitable: A small, terra cotta likeness of the face of some ancient Greek or Roman goddess, formed into a narrow planter. It was installed into the eastern side of the berm and buried enough to be stable but by no means permanent; it is able to be moved (or removed) as the garden evolves.

In its open area I planted *Thymus* 'Ruby Glow', a low growing, spreading thyme with the hope that it would spread and soften the edges of the piece and allow it to further blend into the environment. This remains to be seen.

Easter Sunday, April 12th and the *Iberis* are showing clusters of white flower f ready to bloom. This will be the first plant to flower in the rock garden this year. *Iberis sempervirens* (evergreen candytuft) is in the same family (Brassicaceae) as cabbage, broccoli, mustard, *Alyssum, Nasturtium* and about 100 other genera. It has been naturalized in Utah, North Carolina, Tennessee, Michigan, New York and New Hampshire.

It grows to about 10" tall with evergreen foliage. Mine is the cultivar 'Little Gem' which stays under 6" tall. It self sows freely so flowers should be deadheaded if you don't want new seedlings the following year. In more southern states it often blooms a second time in fall. The plant does require a cool period (40-45 degrees F.) for a month or so in order to flower.

The plant is native to Southern Europe and Western Asia. The genus name *"Iberis"* is named after Iberia, a region in Spain where it is a native to the Iberian Peninsula. The species name *"semperviron"* means "always green", referring to the evergreen foliage.

Mid April and the second plant to show blossoms is the *Armeria* with one pink full flower and other tiny, pink buds showing.

The *Saxifraga* that looked great all winter and leafed out beautifully as spring approached is gone! One evening it was perfect and the next day stolen, as if by a thief in the night! I believe a rabbit to be the culprit but I'll probably never know for sure. It still has some tiny stems showing near the soil line and I'm hoping it will again leaf out. No other plant was touched.

The only hand watering that I have done so far is on the new Thyme planted by the terra cotta sculpture and the "missing" *Saxifraga* in the event the roots will still put out growth. There has been over 3" of rain so far this month, with more coming in the next few days.

The *Calylophus serrulatus* is not showing any new growth at this time and I trimmed off the old, brown stems anyway as they looked unsightly. *Digitalis obscura* (narrow leaf foxglove) is showing new growth within the crown, so I trimmed off all the dead stems from last year. The *Euphorbia x martini* that looked so great all winter has many drooping, dead stems after the last really cold spell and since new growth is showing throughout the crown, I trimmed off all of last year's foliage right down to the crown.

In my herb garden, I have a patch of *Sedum rupestre* 'Angelina', which I divided and added to the rock garden. It has golden "tufted" leaves and tiny yellow flowers in the summer, with the foliage turning more orange than yellow in the fall.

The month of April ended with continued weeding and one application of fish fertilizer on the new plants. The *Iberis* is in full bloom with its white flowers tucked in nicely adjacent to the creeping thyme. The *Phlox subulata* planted earlier this spring is still blooming profusely. *Penstemon mystica* is already over one foot tall and looks really gorgeous with its dark, green foliage tinged with maroon. The *Armeria* is loaded with buds with some pink blossoms showing.

There is no new growth, as yet, on the *Agastache*, nor is there any showing on the *Hymenoxys acaulis*. Both plants look as though they did not survive the winter. The rest of the plants are all showing healthy, new green growth. April was a rainy month (almost five inches) that has helped all of the plants achieve their current condition. If the month had been drier, I would have hand watered all of the plants but this was not necessary.

Figure 15 April in Susan Dana's rock garden.

Figure 16 Susan Dana's rock garden.

Figure 17 Sculpture installed.

Figure 18 Permanent labels.

Figure 19 April view of rock garden from deck.

Figure 20 Rock garden in April after pruning.

CHAPTER 5 MAY

In mid May I visited Mary Tilger's rock garden in Collegeville, P.A. Mary is a Master Gardener and her entire property is a tribute to her gardening expertise. The meticulously mulched and maintained beds, vegetable garden, pond, stream, waterfall and woodland gardens were all carved out of thick, impenetrable woods by Mary herself over the past 16 years.

The rock garden is small, maybe 30' in total length, nestled against a portion of the house and bordered by a walkway to her main entrance. The space originally contained traditional foundation plantings of shrubs that never really did well due to the full sun exposure and excessive heat generated by the walkway and the masonry wall on either side. The plants were all removed and replaced by a rock garden that thrives in the sunny and hot location. This rock garden, according to Mary, proves that in order to have a successful rock garden, one does not need a sloping area or very much space. In fact, she conducts classes on the construction of hypertufa troughs and an entire rock garden could be created on a deck or patio with no available soil at all with her lovely troughs planted with alpine plants.

The subject of the transformation of this space from its original design led Mary to comment that in many cases, rock gardens rarely start out as a rock garden. She also pointed out that a dry spot in full sun where nothing grows well is normally a great spot for a rock garden. We also discussed the subject of drainage and how vital it is for the plants to survive but Mary pointed out that it is in winter that the drainage issue is really the most vital for most rock garden plants as the roots cannot take any excessive moisture and will rot.

This rock garden is filled with many plants that Mary says really just "evolved" without any particular original plan. She lets the plants grow as they will but should they begin to overtake another plant she pulls up a portion, pots them up and gives them away or replants them elsewhere in her surrounding gardens. Should they become too aggressive, they are "yanked out".

The rock garden is totally mulched with a material called "Turface", manufactured by Profile Products LLC (see "Sources" in appendix). It is a product made up of tiny, granulated natural clay particles used on baseball infields around the country. It doesn't break down, resists compaction, drains well, absorbs and retains moisture. The clay is mined in the southern United States.

It is interesting to note that all of the rocks utilized in the rock garden, (and throughout the rest of the gardens), were all obtained from construction sites and local excavation projects, either her own or neighbors.

I particularly liked hearing Mary's gardening philosophy: "Whatever you do, and however you do it, never forget to have fun".

MAY

I love the proximity of the rock garden to my deck at the rear of the house. In all seasons, I find myself often "peeking" out a window to view it, as if something changed since the last time I looked. Perhaps it is because a rock garden is so close to a naturally occurring landscape. My vegetable garden, perennial beds, fruit trees, etc. all seem to me to be a bit contrived although I treat them all with a great deal of love and attention. The rock garden is different; almost as if it has a life of its own.

Rock gardens provide homes for beneficial insects that prey on slugs and snails. Ground beetles, lizards, frogs and toads will find shelter in the rock crevices and also in the stone mulch. An organic gardener can do no better than creating an environment where "problem" organisms are kept in check by natural means. Even slugs and snails are basically beneficial, as they do add organic content to the soil by shredding dead plants into compost. I've never had any luck with traps, beer, etc. and poison baits are hazardous and have no place in a healthy, organic garden (not to mention the world!).

Acquiring and planting seeds is one way to increase the number of plants in any garden rather than obtaining a plant already started. It is one of the various methods of propagation that are discussed in this book and one of the most popular. Seeds are inexpensive, in many cases free and can cover an area efficiently with plant growth. Once the seed is sown, as long as moisture, temperature, air, time and media are in the proper relationship, seedlings will probably emerge.

If seeds are sown in containers, as opposed to planted directly into the garden soil, it is even more important to insure that the seeds and seedlings are kept evenly moist. Also, allow for good air circulation.

When seedlings have developed two or three true leaves, transplant them into a 4" pot.

Fertilize as you would if seedlings were in the ground (review my fertilization schedule in Chapter 3), normally twice a week with fish fertilizer. Once the roots fill the 4" container, the seedling is ready to be transplanted into the garden.

There are some potential problems with seeds that should be noted. First of all, one is really never sure that the new plant springing up from the seed will resemble the parent plant from which it originally came in every aspect. If the seeds were obtained from a professional grower or seed company chances are this will not be a problem. Seeds received as gifts or collected from the wild (even from other gardens) are always suspect.

Also, there is a time issue. Some seeds do not germinate quickly and could even take years, depending on the genus, species or conditions. If planted directly into the garden it is very difficult to keep track of germination. When the new shoots appear in the garden, plant identification could be an issue (are these my new plants or weeds?). Of course, this situation can be avoided by planting the seeds first in pots or other containers.

There is a certain degree of excitement and fun in planting seeds and I wouldn't discourage anyone from planting them. Some tips that may make the process more successful:

1. Make sure the soil or medium in which the seed is to be planted is not compacted. It should be light and airy and well drained for at least a short distance around the planting area.
2. Do _not_ plant many seeds in the same spot. Later, thinning becomes a problem as the young seedlings are easily uprooted. A simple method that works extremely well is to poke a hole into the soil about ½" deep (a finger works well). Fill this void half way with horticultural vermiculite. Try and place one seed (and _only_ one seed) on top of the vermiculite. Now cover the seed with more vermiculite to the surface of the soil.

3. Place your holes as far apart as you would like the actual plants to grow and water slowly and well.
4. Mark the area well. The planted holes will be well visible as the surrounding soil will be a dark brown or black color and each planted hole will be a round circle of a contrasting white or tan color from the vermiculite. Still, add markers of some sort as a reminder of where the seeds were planted. Weeds have a way of creeping in when you are not looking and if some mulch is applied anywhere in the vicinity, your newly planted seeds could easily become lost.
5. Water everyday that it doesn't rain with a traditional watering can (with holes in the spout) so that the water comes out like a gentle rain.
6. When germination occurs and seedlings are clearly visible climbing out of the light colored vermiculite circles, water twice a week with fish fertilizer, following the manufacturer's directions. Use plain water on other days, as needed. Once the plant has grown to the point of having a few sets of leaves, the fish fertilizer can be reduced in accordance with my fertilization schedule in Chapter 3, March.

The month of May is also a great month to be planting in the rock garden. So far, I've added an *Ilex x* 'Rock Garden' and *Sedum spurium* 'Dragon's Blood'. The *Ilex* is a miniature form of holly, recently developed by Rutgers University. It is a tiny plant growing only 4" tall over a ten year period. The tag read "red berries in winter time but very sparse". The *Sedum* is very handsome with its round leaves in a quart pot. It is supposed to bloom all summer "with vibrant, red flowers, growing only 3-4" tall.

Also planted was a *Sedum sexangulare* (Watch chain stone crop) and *Aubrieta heterosis* 'Novalis Blue' (purple rockcress). The *Sedum* has very interesting rounded foliage, thus the common name. The grower's label says the "foliage turns shades of rose and copper in the sun creating a tapestry of color that bursts into brilliant yellow bloom in mid summer". This plant is a low grower, 4-6" tall and a good "spreader" in full sun. The *Aubrieta* is already loaded with blue-purple flowers. I planted it where it will get a bit of shade which it supposedly enjoys.

After the first week of May passed, the rain finally stopped after over 4" measured so far. The sun is out for the first time. The first couple of pink *Saponaria* blossoms are showing with many, many terminal buds tightly closed on the tips of the stems. I'm looking forward to a truly beautiful show of flowers this month. Also, there are 3 or 4 deep lavender-purple flowers on the *Geranium*. In March, I noted that this plant did not look like it survived the winter! Also, more pink *Armeria* flowers are blooming and the *Achillea* has large, white buds, each looking like a miniature cauliflower.

Buds are showing on many other plants. May is surely the month of "awakening" for the rock garden. The *Ceratostigma* is showing fresh, new growth, another plant that I noted in March looked dead.

After another weeding, which is relatively easy after so much rain, I have begun to add new stone mulch for the season. I am using not only the ¾" stone as I did last year but filling in with a smaller, 3/8" stone. The combination looks very good and the smaller stone fills any large openings to prevent weeds and retain moisture throughout the bed.

Mid-May is the time for my first monthly application of compost tea on the rock garden. Compost tea is defined as an aerated solution including beneficial microorganisms from compost combined with other ingredients. According to "Keep It Simple, Inc." (see "sources" in appendix) "it is a concentrated liquid created by a process to increase the numbers of beneficial organisms as an organic approach to plant and soil care". "Keep It Simple, Inc." is the manufacturer of the compost tea I use. Each 5 gallon batch is composed of a mix of compost and microbe food and one batch is sufficient to treat the entire rock garden each month. The compost used contains select wood chips and sawdust, pulverized rock, minerals, fungal ingredients, humus and vermicompost. According to the label there is no "clean green" yard waste, animal manures, soil, sand, dirt or bulking agents. The microbe food contains 80% organic ingredients and 20% natural minerals derived from feather meal, bone meal, cottonseed meal, sulfate of potash-magnesia, alfalfa meal, kelp, soy meal and mycorrhizal.

Since the tea is filled with living beneficial microbes (bacteria and other organisms) it is best sprayed immediately after brewing or at least within 4 hours. The brewing process takes 12 hours of pumped aeration. I set mine up in the evening and let it run all night so I can apply the tea in the morning. The technology of adding air with water and food to make compost tea is relatively new. Historically, compost tea was made by putting compost (or manure and other ingredients) into cheese cloth and letting it soak in water for a few days before application on plants. The aeration process, along with laboratory tested microbe ingredients allows these organisms to multiply at an incredible rate during the brewing process. If manure-based compost is used without sufficient brewing time (oxygenation) the tea could go anaerobic and start brewing unwanted pathogens such as e.coli or salmonella. This is the best reason for buying laboratory tested compost. Very little is needed for a full year's application.

The actual application process is a very pleasant experience for me; very much like watering but slower and easier to study each plant as it gets soaked. The plants are small enough that they get their crowns and roots thoroughly soaked and all the foliage gets a complete foliar spray. I use a pump sprayer with an adjustable nozzle and the entire application process takes me about one hour.

There are lots of blooms in the garden now: *Dianthus* with its "electric" majenta flowers; the newly planted *Aubrieta* with deep purple blossoms; The creeping phlox is still full of pink and pale lavender blooms along side of the *Saponaria* totally covered now with pink flowers; The *Geranium* is also in full bloom, each flower a dark pink and lavender combination looking lovely next to the *Armeria* with its pink "pom-poms" dancing in the late afternoon breeze.

As May draws to a close, there is always weeding to do and I've added more stone mulch here and there as needed. I have hand watered newly added plants but there has been sufficient rainfall for the others. I've added a *Veronica* 'New Century (speedwell) which according to the label is a "new, flowering groundcover that literally covers itself in small blue flowers in late April-May. The evergreen foliage is wonderfully thick and deep green". Also I planted *Arabis caucasica* 'Snowfix' (rockcress) which is normally a plant for hot, windy conditions where many plants wouldn't survive. The label shows a picture of the plant completely covered in white blossoms.

The *Anthemis tinctoria* is now blooming with yellow ray, daisy flowers and the *Penstemon* 'Blue Midnight' is showing it's first pale-purple flower of the season. The *Hymenoxys scarposa* is also blooming with yellow, daisy-like flowers along with the *Genista lydia's* pea-like yellow dainty blossoms on long, wispy stems. The columbine is full of pink and maroon flowers with anthers loaded with yellow pollen. The *Saponaria* continues in full bloom. The blue *Campanula* flowers are stunning next to the deep pink *Dianthus*; A combination sure to be welcomed in any rock garden. The *Dianthus*, or "pinks", as they are usually called, is not named due to their color, even though many cultivars are, in fact, pink. The flower petals do not have a smooth edge but a kind of "fringe" that appears as if they were cut with tiny pinking shears, thus the common name.

May passes this year with almost 6" of rain for the month. Additional irrigation in my garden was not necessary except for the newly added plants. In many parts of the country, especially south and west, hand watering would normally be part of May's garden chores, especially during the hottest days of early spring. The end of the month brings more color to the rock garden. Aside from the blooming plants already mentioned, the *Oenothera* is in rose- pink flower with yellow stamens showing in each center. Also, the *Penstemon pinifolius* 'Nearly Red' has sent up stems to about one foot high and the tubular, pale, reddish-orange drooping blossoms are lovely, surrounded by the foliage of the creeping germander and the Thyme. There is still weeding to be done and more stone mulch required but this month has to be the most pleasant time to do both.

In order to propagate a new plant from an existing one, if you want to insure an exact duplicate, taking a "cutting" is one way to "clone" the parent plant. Much can be written about cuttings, types of cuttings, how much of the stem to include, the efficacy of rooting hormones (which I do <u>not</u> recommend), timing, watering, etc. It is not my intention to use this work as a course in propagation. Basically, a cutting is a piece of a stem, stuck into a growing medium and kept moist (not soggy) until new leaves pop out. It is important to keep the stem cutting "right side up", that is, the bottom end stays down and goes into the medium to root. If you put the original, top end into the soil it will never root. Rooting hormones are used extensively but I do not recommend them ever. They are hazardous to pets and humans, the directions calling for protective gear is scary and most likely, a bit of saliva will work as well as the hormone.

"Division" is another excellent way to create additional plants. Not only is division used to create identical "offspring", it is a sure bet your plants will need dividing at some point even if you don't want more of them. Division will keep rampant growth in check, it will cut down on the size of the foliage making for a healthier plant with more blooms, it will cut down on pest problems and basically, make the plant happier and much better looking.

Division is a simple concept. Dig all around the plant and gradually work it out of the ground with as many roots in tact as possible. Clean off the root ball and cut off the youngest, outside parts of the clump and replant. In replanting a divided clump, treat it as if you were planting a new plant. Add compost to the soil, have a nice hole prepared ahead of time and water the new ("divided") plant well.

Plants root in many different ways and some are easier to divide than others. Once you dig up your plant and inspect the roots, division is a cinch. Some root systems will readily show new plants coming from "runners" (like strawberries) or "offsets" (baby plants) that can be severed and replanted. Some will contain "eyes" that will become buds to form the next new stems and growth (like potatoes). These eyes can be cut off with some roots attached and will re-grow into new plants.

There are lots of theories on when to divide, during what season, before or after flowering, early or late in the day and other considerations. I believe it doesn't matter as long as the divisions are re-planted and cared for as you would any newly acquired plant. Most likely, immediately after blooming would usually be the best time, if possible, so as not to lose an entire flowering season.

Some plants are difficult to divide due to a really thick mass of roots. Also difficult are plants with a small, woody "crown", the spot where the roots join the stems. In this case, "layering" may be a better choice to propagate new offspring. Many plants will "layer" themselves automatically and this is the way they spread in nature.

Layering is simply allowing a longer stem to bend downward where a portion of it is buried in the soil where new roots will form and a new plant is created. *Phlox subulata* or moss phlox is a good example of a rock garden plant where layering works well. When burying the stem, place it in a small hole a few inches wide and not that deep. Place a bent, "u-shaped" wire over the stem ("landscape pins" are sold for this purpose) or place a rock on top to hold it steady in the soil as it grows the new roots. Keep an eye on the watering, as the roots will establish themselves faster during a really dry period. Once stems and flowers develop from the new "offspring", it can be dug up and severed from the original stem and replanted elsewhere in the garden.

Figure 21 Mary Tilger's rock garden.

Figure 22 Genista in May.

Figure 23 Geranium in May.

Figure 24 Saponaria in May.

Figure 25 Armeria in May.

CHAPTER 6 JUNE

In early June I traveled to Huff Church, Pennsylvania to visit Robert Seit on his 189 acre working farm "Lennilea" which includes his nursery. The nursery is comprised of three greenhouses and many beds containing a variety of alpine plants. His rock garden borders a wide path overlooking one of his three ponds below. All of the rocks, many of which are really boulders, he relocated from other areas of the farm with heavy equipment and planted heavily. There are many pathways weaving here and there loaded with thousands of container grown plants, both in sun and shade.

Aside from the container grown plants are shrubs and trees that he started from seed, cuttings or grafts planted throughout the nursery area and beyond. Some are now full size and others newly planted seedlings with every size in between. We took a tour for about an hour and he pointed out so many plants that he has been growing including native Viburnums, redbuds, giant redwoods, pawpaws, Rhododendrons, Cornus and many imported varieties from all over the world. Since 1938 Robert has run his nursery on this property and his knowledge of the plants and their history is astounding. Just outside of the nursery area proper, he has a nut tree orchard taking up about two acres.

There are many varieties of Sedum, Sempervivum, & creeping Thyme along with many plants that I couldn't identify tucked into the crevices of the rocks. At least the container plants and all the greenhouse plants were labeled simply with a pencil on white plastic markers. He makes up his entire soil medium himself, using a local quarry stone called "Gneiss" which is ground into yellow, coarse sand and gravel and mixed with pine bark and 20% top soil. He likes this sand and gravel mixture for rock gardens as it is on the acid side.

I thoroughly enjoyed my visit to this lovely and picturesque farm and Robert's kind manner. I left with a Sedum hispanicum for my own rock garden and a gift of a Silene seedling of an unknown origin.

JUNE

One of the first rock garden chores for June is pruning back the earlier spring flowering plants. In the case of my own garden, the *Phlox subulata* is ready. The blossoms are pretty much gone and the pruning technique is similar to many other plants and simple. I use small scissors and clip away the perimeter of each plant, along with the top until only about 1/3rd of the original plant is left. The cuttings are placed in the compost and the pruning takes only minutes. *Dianthus* pruning is similar and can be done also at this time. Any plants still blooming profusely should be left alone.

Some of the early blooms in the June garden are *Penstemon x mexicale* 'Red Rocks' with pink, trumpet-like flowers nodding up and down the stem. There are lots of buds showing on the *Penstemon* 'Mystica'. The *Digitalis obscura* is showing its first spike of orange-yellow tubular flowers. *Calylophus serrulatus* is full of yellow blossoms. *Achillea x* 'Moonshine' is showing yellow buds in the "cauliflower-like" flower clusters that were evident in May. The *Aubrieta heterosis* is showing one lavender blossom.

Scarlet pimpernel (*Anagallis arvensis*) is an annual weed that tries to take over my rock garden in June. Part of the Primrose family (Primulaceae), it is easy to pull and low-growing so it's more of an annoyance than a threat to other plants. It looks similar to common chickweed but chickweed has round stems and the scarlet pimpernel stems are square. Also, chickweed has white flowers where the scarlet pimpernel flowers are orange. Scarlet pimpernel leaves have tiny purplish dots on their undersides which chickweed leaves do not. Since it reproduces by seed, it is best to pull it out before or during flowering.

For the majority of rock garden plants, although the drainage, specific soil composition and availability of water are major factors in their survival, temperature is probably the most critical.

The number one guide throughout the country to plant hardiness is the United States Department of Agriculture's Hardiness Zone Map (www.USNA.USDA/hardzone/). This map is based upon the range of minimum temperatures within a certain zone that would indicate the limits of a plant's ability to survive a winter season. There is a ten-degree "spread" in temperature for each zone. In my zone 6 garden the "spread" is zero degrees to minus ten degrees Fahrenheit.

Gardeners must keep two things in mind about this "hardiness zone" concept. First of all, many monitoring thermometers throughout a region, indicating a season's minimum temperature at any instant in time, for any duration, establish the minimum temperatures.

For example, assume the minimum temperature from December through the end of January reached ten degrees and remained there for some time. Then, one night in February, the temperature spiked for just an instant to eight degrees. The new minimum for that season (or year) would now be eight degrees. This minimum temperature of eight degrees would now be averaged with all the past years' minimum temperatures to arrive at the "Minimum Average" temperature for the zone.

As you can see, any zone's spread in temperature could be influenced one way or another by an unusual cold snap at just an instant in time. Again, my zone 6 temperature spread is zero degrees to minus ten degrees yet the temperature has not hit zero (the top of the range) in at least the past eight years. I don't remember the temperature hitting the lowest end (minus ten degrees) in decades.

Therefore, use these zones as a guide but don't be afraid to experiment with plants listed out of your particular zone. In my zone 6 garden I have many plants growing well, listed as zone 7 plants. I have even had zone 8 plants come back in the spring from under a coating of thick, winter mulch.

The second thing to consider is that in every zone "microclimates" can occur within any area, which can substantially alter your USDA zone category. If your rock garden is sheltered somewhat by structures or dense trees, is located at the bottom of a hill, receives plenty of reflected winter sun or many, many other factors all help in creating these microclimates.

One simple way to monitor a microclimate would be to place a minimum/maximum thermometer near your rock garden to see if there is a higher or lower temperature range as distinguished from somewhere else on your property.

Don't be afraid to experiment here and there with plants outside of your zone. Aside from the fun of trying different species think of the design potential possible with so many more plants able to be installed.

After the middle of June, all plants that survived the winter should be growing well, have full foliage (if not blooms yet) and many will need thinning or cutting back. In my garden, after a very rainy June, the creeping thymes need to be cut back to keep from spreading over neighboring plants. *Thymus serpyllum* especially and also the *Thymus* 'Ruby Glow' planted at my sculpture. They are easily "snipped" with scissors to keep them in line where necessary. Both are just beginning to bloom now. The *Gaura* is beginning its summer "show" with pink flowers looking lovely next to the blue *Campanula* which is still in bloom since the spring. The lavender is in full purple bloom with lots of bees "working the blossoms". The *Sedum spurium* 'Dragon's Blood' is showing deep, pink-red flowers here and there. The *Armeria* is showing many spent blossoms and is cut back (deadheaded) to the foliage below. The *Sedum sexangulare* is spreading slowly and packed with tiny, star-like yellow flowers. The *Anthemis tintoria* is showing many yellow, daisy-like flowers and many are in need of deadheading. The stems are cut as low as possible to the base of the plant. The *Digitalis*, just since early June is now blooming profusely along with its neighbors *Calylophus serrulatus* and *Achillea*. The yellow blossoms are gorgeous next to the blue blooms of *Penstemon*.
The *Agastache* 'Salmon & Pink' that was so pretty last year never re-sprouted after the winter and so I removed the crown. *Agastache,* a southwest native plant is not only hardy but normally very adaptable to various climates. Most species bloom until a hard frost. The plants do not like moist winter soil and are short-lived in damp, cool climates. Perhaps more rock mulch would have provided the required drainage and saved the plant? The two *Sempervivum* are sending up high flower

clusters (chicks?) 6" tall right from the center of each plant. The blood grass is showing its crimson-maroon blades and they look great waving in the summer breeze. The *Teucrium* is spreading at the border. The *Penstemon* 'Mystica' is high, in full flower and may have to be relocated to a perennial bed. It is looking too large for the scale of the rock garden. The *Saponaria* has only a few pink blossoms left and will soon have to be trimmed back.

Weeding is easier now but still needs to be done here and there, along with replenishing the stone mulch. The June application of compost tea has been done and fish fertilizer should continue to be used on new cuttings, seeds or plants as added prior to the end of summer. The fish fertilizer that I use is "Neptune's Harvest", a product made by Ocean Crest Seafood's, Inc. in Gloucester, MA. It is certified organic by OMRI (Organic Materials Review Institute) and contains only fresh, North Atlantic fish remains. It is a 2-4-1 fertilizer (2% Nitrogen, 4% Phosphorus and 1% Potassium by weight). According to the company, aside from the NPK contents, the mixture contains naturally occurring vitamins, minerals, macro and micro nutrients, amino acids, trace elements and growth hormones. No oil or meal is removed from the fish and it is not cooked. The label says "no unpleasant odor". I've used this product for years, love the results but for the first 15 minutes after application, it smells like fish!

The company also makes a fish and seaweed mixture and a seaweed only mixture, made from kelp. The seaweed "plant food" is a 0-0-1 fertilizer containing only 1% of the product's weight in soluble potassium. Although potassium (or "potash") is good for a plant's overall health, I believe that the fish fertilizer alone contains a sufficient amount for each application.

June is a good month to make notes on areas that could use additional plants and also noting color combinations, as there are so many plants in flower at this time.

In areas of the country where there has not been at least an inch of rainfall per week, supplemental watering may be required this month.

It is important to water only once a week and deeply so that the roots will seek new depths and the plants will be stronger. This is a much better strategy than watering more often with a shallow soaking.

At the end of June I relocated the two plants that I thought were getting too large for the scale of my garden. The *Penstemon* 'Mystica' that I discussed earlier in this chapter and *Caryopteris x clandonensis* 'Longwood Blue' mentioned in MARCH have both been relocated to a nearby perennial bed.

Once you confirm that any particular plant no longer "works" in its space, for whatever reason, it is best to remove it before it spreads too much and the roots find their way throughout those of neighboring plants. I decided to "act" on these two plants at this time as with the approaching heat of July and August, successful transplanting becomes more difficult.

Figure 26 Robert Seit's Alpine plants.

Figure 27 Robert Seit's Rock garden.

Figure 28 Anthemis tinctoria 'Susanna Mitchell'.

Figure 29 Aquilegia x caerulea 'Red Hobbit'.

Figure 30 Calylophus serrulatus with lavender.

Figure 31 Geranium sanguineum 'Max Frei'.

Figure 32 Rock garden in June.

CHAPTER 7 JULY

In late July I visited the Morris Arboretum of the University of Pennsylvania in Chestnut Hill, Pennsylvania. It was very hot but a beautiful, sunny, summer day. The rock garden is very unique in that it is a vertical rock wall about five feet high and about 500 feet long bordering their rose garden on three sides. The wall was constructed around 1920 and originally planted over 80 years ago. There are many hundreds of plants tucked into the stone crevices. Most are not labeled and not pruned, left to cascade as they will, forming a tapestry of textures and colors throughout the entire length of the wall.

The plants consist of many types of ferns, Salvias, Geraniums, Sedums, thymes, Dianthus, Sempervivum, Vinca, Aurinia, Corydalis, and Arabis to name some of the major groups. Many were in bloom with a variety of purple, pink and yellow flowers accenting the varied foliage. Although the vertical rock wall formed the base of the garden itself, most was covered by the plants with bare stone only showing here and there to remind a visitor of the structure they were actually seeing.

A vertically planted surface does work in certain situations and has been successfully installed in a variety of gardens. The difficult part is to not have the finished project look "contrived" and "sticking out" in a manner to draw attention to it. This wall is a perfect example of how to create a rock garden as an understated, vertical border to the surrounding landscape. A similar situation could be installed as a low wall bordering a pond or water feature, as a transition between various heights in the natural landscape (perhaps a retaining wall) and also adjacent to stone steps as one moves from one garden area (or "room") to another.

JULY

A beautiful summer July morning with clear skies, 65 degrees and a nice breeze; a perfect day for weeding, mulching and trimming. Robert Seit's *Silene* is in full bloom with pinwheel, "electric" pink flowers.

The *Armeria* blossoms have faded and all stems are cut back at this time to the foliage below. Don't be concerned about clipping some of the grass-like foliage also; it will fill in nicely as the summer progresses.

As I work my way around the garden, weeding as needed, I also fill in with stone mulch only where there are obvious voids. The beauty of the stone mulch, aside from how it looks, holds moisture in the soil and keeps weeds down, is that it doesn't decompose and lasts from season to season..

The *Anthemis tinctoria* has spread its stems in about a four foot diameter so even though it is still in bloom with many white daisies blooming, many of the spreading stems can be cut back now to shape the plant and remove the spent blossoms. Any dead, brown stems are also cut off near the bottom of the plant.

The *Euphorbia x martini* has come back beautifully after its winter die-back. It is shapely and in full foliage without any need to prune. It is truly a remarkable plant and highly recommended.

The Hens and chicks are both showing long flower stalks from the center of the plant and blossoming with a myriad of pink flower clusters.
Although most rock garden plants are not prone to disease, it is possible for some plants to succumb, especially if drainage is not as it should be, air circulation is not adequate or if there is just too much moisture and humidity.

"Powdery mildew" is one that may appear on the leaves of some plants if the nights are cool and humid followed by warm, dry days. It becomes clearly visible as a white or gray powdery fungus coating, usually on the top of the leaves. These fungi are parasites, requiring live tissue to grow and reproduce. The spores are carried by air currents and germinate on leaf surfaces. It can spread in dry weather, as it doesn't need water to germinate, usually just a bit of shade. The disease is caused by a variety of different types of fungi. This means that the powdery mildew on one plant may not necessarily be caused by the same organism as that on another.

Prevention is possible if watering can be accomplished without wetting the foliage, which is difficult, if not impossible without the use of soaker hoses. At least, watering in the early morning allowing the sun to dry the leaves is best. Powdery mildew can cause poor growth but it seldom kills the plant. It is common on many garden plants not normally found in a rock garden and ultimately goes away without causing permanent damage. During the winter, the fungus can survive on infected plant parts such as fallen leaves and certain weeds, so it's best to weed, clean up and discard debris if powdery mildew was present. Overall, the disease is usually more of a concern to the gardener than the plant. Try not to pay too much attention to it.

In the event that you would like a remedy for getting rid of the unsightly white coating, spraying with sulfur can be effective. Also, spraying with a garlic solution can help. Crush a few cloves in water, strain and spray. Garlic actually contains sulfur, probably why this application works. There is a spray treatment developed by Cornell University in Ithaca, New York that has proven very effective. Actually, one treatment could be enough for an entire gardening season. The ingredients are as follows:

- (1) Gallon of water
- (2) Tablespoons of light horticultural oil
- (1) Heaping teaspoon of baking soda
- (1) Tablespoon of mild dishwashing detergent

Mix all the ingredients well and spray with a pump-up sprayer late in the evening when the sun is no longer shining on the foliage. Spray both sides of the leaves and all the stems until the solution is running off. Make sure the plants are well irrigated, at least a day before spraying.

Care should be taken by the organic gardener to obtain products that are certified "organic" as many available products are not. "OMRI" stands for "Organic Materials Review Institute" and their stamp of approval is one way to insure what you are using is an organic product.

For the recipe above, the sources listed in the appendix can supply the required organic products. "Baking soda" requires a bit more explanation. Baking soda is actually "sodium bicarbonate". Although it is non-toxic, it is not a product that occurs in nature; that is, it must be refined and consequently not considered an organic product. Some alternatives to consider are:

1. Armicarb 100, available from Helena Chemical Company.
2. Kaligreen, available from Peaceful Valley Farm Supply.
3. FirstStep, available from W.A. Cleary Chemical Company.
4. Remedy, available from Gardener's Supply Company.

I do not consider myself a garden designer, nor do I consider myself a plant collector. I don't mind at all a single plant, placed into the rock garden that "looks right". This "looking right" is based solely upon my own aesthetic considerations and what pleases me. I am not concerned with "grouping by threes", "proper" color coordination or the like. Many gardeners may not admit it but I believe this "what I like" mentality to be more the norm than garden journals and magazines would suggest. That being said, I do believe that understanding some basic terminology and characteristics of the design process can be a big help when actually working on your own rock garden.

The "design" of a rock garden has wide parameters. The gardener may want to re-create a small scale "model" of an actual alpine landscape or simply tend a garden of a smaller scale, utilizing rocks in the landscape and smaller plants that suit his or her fancy.
Reginald Farrer in his classic work "The English Rock Garden" states that under no circumstances should a rock garden be located near "trees or bushes of any sort" and must be in an "open" site. I can

assure you that this advice, given in 1913, was purely his opinion and not valid in many, many circumstances today.

In my own rock garden, the overhanging cherry tree provides a bit of most welcome shade in the hot summer months for many of the plants and the pink blossoms in spring form a spectacular canopy over the emerging rock garden plants. He also said that the "rock-garden should not be near a wall, a border, a formal path, a house; or within sight of any such regular and artificial construction." This direction may have had some merit at the end of the nineteenth century in England but doesn't work at all in the United States in the twenty first century. The rock gardens of today can easily be blended into any of these "artificial constructions" efficiently and aesthetically.

I am in total agreement with his rock garden design advice when he discusses imitating nature (as many rock gardening authors have written about): "To make a thing look 'natural' is by no means to imitate nature. Nature often looks more artificial than the worst forms of artificial art; nature in the mountains is often chaotic, bald, dreary and hideous in the highest degree. By making a rock-garden look natural, then, we merely mean that it must have a firm and effortless harmony……..''

In any case, the actual design process with regard to a rock garden does not have to be a difficult process. The available, potential garden space is what forms the basis of the ultimate design.

Soil type, exposure to wind, sun, shade and other existing landscape features must be considered. In many cases (if not most) a rock garden begins simply where the space is available. Obviously, the larger the property the more potential locations exist but most people have smaller lots and rock gardens lend themselves to areas where trees, shrubbery or traditional perennial beds or cutting gardens don't work.

Once the rock garden space is confirmed, "scale" must be considered. The term "scale" in this regard refers to the proportion between sets of dimensions. The ultimate size of the plants in conjunction with the size of the rocks would be an example. Tiny, prostrate plants and large boulders normally are out of scale as would be fist sized stones and plants the size of dwarf trees.

Along with scale, "balance" is an element of the overall design. Balance is created by one part of the garden being of equal visual weight or mass to another part. This concept can be pictured as a seesaw with a large adult on one end. On the other end could be another large adult (balance) or perhaps a few small children (again, balance). If the balance is symmetrical, the rock garden will have a more formal look. This symmetrical balance is the creation of an axis where everything on one side is duplicated or mirrored on the other side. Asymmetrical balance is achieved by using different objects to create equilibrium; perhaps a larger rock on one side and a grouping of many plants on the other to counterbalance it. Most rock gardens tend to be asymmetrical by nature.

The design concept of "unity" needs to be utilized in almost all garden designs except in the rock garden. The use of too many accent plants with a variety of foliage types, colors and sizes in a small area normally would not result in a pleasant design, say in a perennial bed. It would be better to group similar plants together to appear as single "units" here and there. In the rock garden, due to the predominately small sizes of plants, I believe the more variety, the more interesting the entire garden space becomes. I never tire of seeing the "dance" of colors, textures and shapes in my own, or any other rock garden.

As the plants grow and fill out they tend to blend together in what appears to be more of a woven tapestry than a group of different plants. One could argue that this ultimate "woven tapestry" of plants is, in fact, unity. All I can say is that I love seeing it and I do believe that it is one of the desired results of rock garden design.

After so much rain through the spring season, mid July finally brought dry and hot weather. For the first time this year I had to water (except, of course, for newly installed plants) and I let the sprinkler do the soaking for a good three hours. It is always better to thoroughly soak the garden extremely well, if needed, once a week than a shallow watering more often. This fact cannot be repeated enough and works for most gardening situations, especially vegetables and perennials.

This month I planted new plants in the spaces where the larger ones were previously removed. *Alyssum montanum* 'Mountain Gold', an early bloomer in mid spring with "masses of fragrant gold flowers" according to the label was planted on the east side of my bed. The foliage on this plant is very interesting. The leaves are long and narrow, 3-4" in length and very "soft looking". From a short distance they almost resemble *Stachys byzantina* (lambs-ears) with narrower leaves.

Also planted were (3) stonecrops: *Sedum reflexum* 'Blue Spruce', *Sedum spurium* 'John Creech' and *Sedum spurium* 'Tricolor'. The *Sedum reflexum* has spruce-like foliage pointing out in all directions and is just starting to show yellow flower buds. The 'Tricolor' has foliage that is variegated-green paddle-like leaves with white edges and already showing many pink flower buds. The 'John Creech' has foliage more like a typical Sedum with tiny, whorled, round green leaves with no hint of flowers or buds.

Whenever a new plant is installed, I try to leave at least a foot or more empty space around their perimeter to allow for spread.

Figure 33 Right rock wall at Morris Arboretum.

Figure 34 Left rock wall at Morris Arboretum.

Figure 35 Close up of rock wall at Morris Arboretum.

Figure 36 July rock garden.

Figure 37 Sempervivum 'Red Beauty' in flower.

Figure 38 Sempervivum dual flowers.

Figure 39 West rock garden in July.

CHAPTER 8 AUGUST

Wave Hill is a beautiful, public, 28-acre garden high on a hillside, overlooking the Hudson River in the Riverdale section of the Bronx, New York City. My August visit was on a warm, lovely summer day. The rock garden is comprised of an alpine glass house and an outdoor terrace, the highest of three levels. The garden is constructed with concrete and stone planters filled with alpine plants along with many other types of planted containers of various sizes and shapes. The garden is bordered by a stone wall and on the opposite side of the garden is a bed planted with a variety of small trees (Locusts and Junipers) providing areas of shade over half of the garden. The rock wall itself is a vertical tapestry of alpine plants flowing in all directions.

The plantings are grouped in a very picturesque manner, with a great diversity of foliage and flowers. This design creates a unified theme throughout the entire garden. Many of the planted groupings are extremely miniature in nature and unlabeled. Some of the larger groupings included Potentilla alchemilloides, Artemisia assoana, Saponaria x olivana and a dwarf Chamaecyparis pisifera all planted together in a two foot square planter.

Another similar planter contained Globularia cordifolia nana, Prunus pumila and Thymus praecox minor spreading throughout and draping over the edges. Many plantings were both evergreen and herbaceous. A dwarf Juniperus chinensis 'Shimpaku' with Gypsophila bungeana, Ulmus parvifolia 'Hokkaido' with Saponaria pumila, Ilex crenata 'Dwarf Pagoda' with Alyssoides utriculata and one containing a lovely Cryptomeria japonica 'Tenzan' surrounded by Silene alpestris and Artemisia 'Little Green' to name just a few examples.

I left the garden in the late afternoon very stimulated with a strong desire to add more dwarf evergreens to my own garden.

AUGUST

A small rock garden is fine, especially in dry periods where some watering is required. I like the fact that large areas of natural rock outcrops can be duplicated in miniature in my own garden. So far this season, in my Pennsylvania location, watering has not been an issue due to unusually high rainfall. I'm sure this is not the case in other areas around the country, especially the south, southwest and California in many areas. August brings the heat and drought to the Northeast. The temperature approaches the high 90's, the sun bakes the ground and whatever mulch is used is generally not sufficient to prevent hand watering. Watering should be at least once a week, slowly and deeply. Use a can, a sprinkler, a hose or whatever device you have and make sure the ground is truly soaked. With the excellent drainage that all rock gardens require, over-watering should never be an issue.

Watch your plants closely during these hot summer days. A little dark sun scorch spot could develop on some foliage, leaf edges could become a bit yellow or brown and the foliage can begin to wilt. The trick here is to water *before* the signs actually show on the plants. Once a plant is wilted from dryness it can recover quickly from a good "drink" but it has been stressed and that is not a good thing. Insects and disease generally will attack a stressed plant as opposed to one that is healthy. This fact is not a truism and can't be stated for all plants.

Water when it is required and when you are able. Morning watering is said by many gardeners to be the best as the plant has a chance to dry prior to lower evening temperatures that could attract fungus. Evening watering is also acceptable, as the sun is not evaporating the surface moisture as it does when watering occurs in mid-day. In any case, don't worry! When watering is required, do it whenever you can, regardless of the time of day.

When maintaining any garden, it is a good idea to have some knowledge about insects in general and the variety of pollinators, especially bees. Insects belong in our gardens. We would all be better off to learn to attract them than to spend the time and money that many gardeners do to repel them. A garden really wouldn't be a garden without them. There are millions of species in the world and many will be in our gardens; thousands of them at any time. Some can be seen easily and many cannot be seen with the naked eye. Most of them (but not all) can fly. Every one of them originated from an egg that was laid somewhere in the garden, in many cases on a specific "host" plant. Please forget about "controlling" these creatures with sprays, chemicals and poisons that garden centers are loaded with. Our gardens do not need poisons and with a bit of understanding of unique life styles one can readily learn to appreciate how nature works in the garden.

In themselves, insects are not "good" or "bad", "pests" or "beneficials". They are simply living their lives in an effort to survive and reproduce themselves. They are, for the most part, simply "doing their thing" in our gardens.

We love birds in our gardens. Most of our favorites eat insects. Thousands of insects are constantly recycling organic material directly in the garden soil itself. Insects carry out the bulk of the pollination of our flowers. Many rock garden plants reproduce themselves without pollination but most flowers are the result of the insect's work. The more diversely our gardens are planted, the more we can look forward to attracting and sheltering the myriad of insects that will keep our gardens somewhat in balance.

Buy a magnifying glass and use it often to see what insects are living in your plants. As Louis Agassiz has written, "Study nature, not books! Watch your plants!"

Be especially grateful for spiders in your garden (although these are not insects). They are continually eating insects that could eventually cause some degree of harm to your plants.

Of all the insects found in the garden, aside from the beautiful butterflies, my favorites are the bees. Many of these bees are "solitary", unlike the hive dwelling honeybees that most people are familiar with. These solitary bees are great pollinators, don't really bother humans and nest in a great variety of invisible places throughout the garden. The great variety of flowering plants in the rock garden will attract them. They are constantly looking for pollen that they line their nests with and lay their eggs in.

There are 40,000 species of bees worldwide. Of that total, about 4,000 are native to the United States. Each state has a varying amount of native bees. Pennsylvania has 450 and California has 1,400, for example. It is interesting to note that out of the 40,000 species only seven are honeybees. The United States has only one species of honeybee and it is not a native to our country. Bees are vegetarians. Pollen is their only source of proteins. Wasps are carnivores and get their protein from other insects (although they eat nectar also). Wasps have little or no hair and unlike bees, their markings are on their exoskeleton and not in the hairs like bees. Of all the bees, only the females sting.

When identifying bees, remember that they all have 4 wings, as opposed to flies that have only 2. Also, flies have big eyes and short antennae plus their wings are always out sideways. Bees have long antennae and are covered in hair. Bees cannot "hover" like flies. In many cases, bee species are very difficult to positively identify. Some bees that may be encountered in any garden include carpenter bees. The males are very aggressive and can be seen chasing each other but can't sting. They don't have much color; a pretty shiny, huge black abdomen and a yellow thorax (the part between the neck and the abdomen).

 The males have a vertical, yellow stripe on their face. Bumblebees are the same large size as carpenter bees but they are very hairy and very yellow (head, thorax and abdomen). Cuckoo bees look like wasps, are bright, metallic green, very "pitted" and they lay their eggs in other nests of bees. Leaf cutter bees and mason bees are very similar. They create a consistent "notch" in a leaf but it doesn't hurt the plant. They like grape hyacinths in spring. The males have a white moustache. They look like small honeybees but they collect pollen on the hairs of their belly, not on their legs as a honeybee does. The mason bees get their name as they work with mud to build and seal their nests. They are not aggressive and won't ever sting unless severely provoked.

The largest bee you will probably see is the giant resin bee. It has a very large head and jaws. Sweat bees are very tiny and have a metallic coloring. Most nest in the ground. Squash bees are usually found around squash plants but they are only seen in the morning, usually up to 10:00 AM. Finally, mining bees look like small bumblebees. They are the biggest bees in the spring. There are many, many others and only with appropriate guidebooks (and the Internet) and incredible patience can their true identity be confirmed. Again, they are all beneficial and should be welcomed in any garden.

August weeding and mulching continues along with another application of compost tea. There is lots of color in the garden at this time. The plumbago is in full blue bloom with flowers spreading neatly around the plant. The *Aconitum* has a few lingering blue blossoms. The *Sedum spurium* 'Dragon's Blood' has a few deep red blossoms along with a few pink-lavender flowers on the *Geranium*. Many yellow blossoms are spread around the garden on the *Anthemis, Achillea,* and both *Hymenoxys acaulis* and *H.scaposa.* The *Penstemon* 'Blue Midnight' is covered with purple flowers, the *Gaura* with pink and the *Origanum* 'Rotkugel' with tiny pink flowers spreading on long stems in all directions. Pink *Dianthus* blossoms complete the color palate along with the *Penstemon* 'Red Rocks' lovely pink, tubular blossoms.

Looking closely at this particular *Penstemon*, the stems have many large, empty insect skins attached where the adults exited. These are the nymphal skins shed by cicadas. Cicadas develop underground, sucking sap from the roots of various plants. Normally, they require years to complete their life cycle. They have the longest life of any insect. The nymphs emerge from the soil (some species after 13 or 17 years) in late May or early June and climb onto stems, like my *Penstemon*, shed their skin and move up into the trees. The males produce that familiar, loud summer "buzzing" sound to attract females. They mate in the trees and the female deposits her eggs into branches and twigs. When the eggs hatch, the nymphs drop to the ground, move into the soil and feed on roots. The most amazing thing about these cicadas is that somehow, all of the nymphs escape and become adults *at exactly the same time!*

Very little trimming of plants is required at this time of the year, other than dead branches or leaves and perhaps some deadheading. August is the hottest month of the year in Zone 6 and most other zones as well. An eye must be kept out for water requirements as this is also traditionally a dry month. Especially needy are any newly installed plants that are not yet fully established. All of my *Sedums* are spreading about happily with lush, compact and varied foliage types. This genus is definitely my most favorite for any rock garden.

As the month ends, the *Dianthus* continues to bloom, along with some *Campanula* blossoms. The Plumbago (*Ceratosigma plumbaginoides*) has spread to about a four foot diameter and is still loaded with pure blue flowers. The *Penstemon x mexicale* 'Red Rocks' has also spread to about a three foot canopy with pink blooms here and there. The *Sedum spurium* 'Dragon's Blood' still has a few red blossoms but that's the only *Sedum* showing color. *Hymenoxys acaulis* has a few yellow daisies showing and the *Gaura* some pink blooms and that is it for the "end of summer" color.

Due to the unusual amount of August rain (13 inches) there has been little need to water the rock garden and except for new plants ordered for the fall, no more water should be called for. There will be some fall trimming, a bit of weeding and additional stone mulch as required. This is the time to enjoy the garden as the colors change and it begins the slow decent into dormancy. This is also the time to order (or at least get out the summer notes of plants that we would like to install this fall). Fall is an excellent time to plant. The days are mild and the nights cool which help the new roots grow, especially with some rainfall that is common at this time throughout most of the country. Many nurseries stock perennial plants at this time suitable for rock gardens and catalogs are abundant. Refer to the source list in the appendix.

Figure 40 Sedum reflexum 'Blue Spruce' in August.

Figure 41 Ceratostigma plumbaginoides (plumbago) in August.

Figure 42 Wave Hill rock garden (left).

Figure 43 Wave Hill rock garden (center).

Figure 44 Wave Hill rock garden (right side).

CHAPTER 9 SEPTEMBER

On a September morning in 1993, my son Daniel and I backpacked up Snowmass Mountain in Aspen, Colorado. We set up a base camp at 11,000 feet next to the lake, slightly below the timberline. Each morning, for the next three days, we hiked up to the summit of a different 14,000-foot peak in the surrounding area.

On our last morning, in bright sunshine, we were close to the top of one of these peaks, well above any vegetation, on a rock-strewn, very steep path. As we progressed, ever so slowly due to the thin air, I spotted ahead in a rock crevice a lovely, yellow-blooming, alpine plant. It was the perfect natural rock garden environment for this small, low-growing and healthy specimen.

I could not identify the plant. There was no camera or sketchpad so we tried to commit to memory as many of its features as possible. After looking through many, many reference books, regional guidebooks and countless websites I am still unable to identify that plant.

Over a decade has past since that incident and I've never seen the plant again. My memory is perhaps a bit blurry on the plant's specific features but not it's environment. I remember so well that rock crevice and the way the plant was growing. It comes to mind often as I work in my own rock garden.

SEPTEMBER

Labeling plants in a rock garden is a rather controversial subject. This statement is mainly due to the size of the plants in relation to the size of the labels. Vegetables, perennials, shrubs or trees can be labeled in an inconspicuous manner but rock garden labels are always very visible.

Some feel that the labels spoil the natural quality and "look" of the rock garden setting. Others complain that the labels themselves create a "congested" landscape in some ways resembling a "tiny cemetery".

My rock garden is labeled and I would have it no other way. As a matter of fact, I've spent so much time in public gardens and arboretums that when I visit a garden without labels I feel somewhat cheated. I am referring here to cultivated and well-maintained garden spaces as opposed to meadow-like and other naturally planted areas.

Whenever a plant or seedling is planted, my "initial" label goes in at the same time. I have tried all types of available labels of various materials such as wood, plastic and metal. For my purposes, the metal, two-part labels work the best (see "A.M. Leonard" in sources). I use an indelible pen with black ink, slide the horizontal label onto the 2-prong stake and install the label somewhere in front of the plant.

I called the above labeling "initial" because it is not the permanent label that I use. After one year of healthy growth and survival of an entire winter and summer season, each plant gets a professionally engraved arboretum-style plastic label (see "Gardenmarkers.com" in sources). These labels are horizontal, approximately 1" deep by 3" wide with the plant name showing white against the label's black background. The label is attached to the metal stake with an adhesive backing and the stake is pushed into the soil so that the label is a bit higher than the top of the mulch. It looks nice, does not seem obtrusive and lasts if not forever, certainly longer than the gardener installing it.

Some gardeners who also use metal labels use a standard #2 pencil as opposed to the indelible black pen. The writing does not seen to fade away as the indelible pen will do in time. My problem with the pencil is that I can't read it from any distance and I need to crawl almost on top of the label to make it out.

I have not found the fading of the black ink a problem. The benefit of reading it so easily is a plus and anyway it is replaced the next year with a permanent label as long as the plant survives. The metal "initial" labels are saved and reused as needed. Most gardeners don't know that the indelible ink can be removed by rubbing the label with your fingers and a bit of any standard machine lubricating oil.

Engraved metal labels are used by some gardeners, which are extremely long lasting but equally hard to read without getting as close as you would to read a book. I find them annoying, especially in the rock garden environment, where they remind me of military dog tags. By the way, over time they will rust and become even harder to read.

The benefit of a label "program" allows the gardener to be reminded at a glance of where specific plants were originally planted and how they have spread. Also, it clearly shows which plants are thriving as opposed to those that may not have survived a particular season. The benefit to visitors, both horticulturally and educationally, goes without saying.

Finally, there is the simple "memory function". Gardeners sometimes forget what was planted where. Also, many times early spring shoots cannot readily be confirmed as plant or weed. Finally, there could always be a question if no label exists, if a current bare spot was ever actually planted.

In early September I started my fall planting with two dwarf evergreens, inspired by my visit to Wave Hill Garden last month. The first, a *Chamaecyparis pisifera* 'Tsukumo', which is a miniature Swara Cypress. The plant is labeled to grow only one inch a year. The second, a *Chamaecyparis obtuse* 'Nana Gracilis'.

This dwarf Hinoki Cypress is very popular in today's marketplace and looks lovely with its intense, dark green foliage. They were both planted in full sun on the southwestern edge of the garden.

If every organic gardener worldwide had one trait in common, it would be that they all make compost. It could be said that the addition of compost to any garden soil is the essence of the organic garden. Although rock gardens in general don't need a highly rich, organic soil, they all benefit from the addition of compost whenever it is available. Compost helps to aerate the soil, providing home to millions of living organisms that assist in a plant's ability to take up required nutrients. In that sense, it acts as a fertilizer. Actually, with enough compost added to garden soil on a regular basis, no additional fertilizer or "plant food" would ever be required. The compost could be used as mulch, spread on top of the existing soil as often as possible and certainly mixed with the existing soil when installing new plants.

Compost is easy to make. It is simply the end result of a pile of organic matter decomposing into a rich, chocolate-brown material that looks good, smells good, feels good to touch and is often referred to as "black gold" by gardeners worldwide. Technically, compost will result from a combination of any once-living organic material, either animal or vegetable. It all decomposes in time. The modern day compost pile does not use animal material and due to antibiotics and other medications given to many farm animals, even manure is not always recommended for a compost pile. Should manure be available from organically raised farm animals, it can be safely added to any compost pile. However, raw, or "fresh" manure should never be added directly to any garden bed.

A compost pile or "heap" can be created anywhere a four foot by four foot section of earth is available. It can be located in the shade, in the sun, in a dry area, a damp area, virtually anywhere. Simply toss your organic material on the ground, building up a pile to four feet high and given enough time, underneath it all you will find compost.

Weeds, leaves, kitchen scraps (don't include meat or dairy products), coffee grounds, over-ripe fruit, tea bags, nut shells, seaweed, pine needles, sawdust, human or animal hair clippings and the list goes on and on. It will all decompose into perfect compost.

Should a neater look be desired, an actual bin can be constructed, preferably two or three adjacent to one another. Any material that would keep your organic "litter" contained will work. A wire cage, scrap lumber, concrete masonry block, old pallets, just about anything will work.

Some tips on composting would be:

1. Try to chop or shred your debris as small as possible. The smaller the particles, the faster the decomposition.
2. Try to layer the material as much as possible. Cover kitchen scraps with a layer of shredded leaves, for example. Even a shovelful of soil works as a layer. Alternate material within the pile as much as possible.
3. Keep the pile damp, not soggy. The dampness of a wrung-out sponge is about right.
4. Aerate the pile from time to time. Turning it over with a pitchfork or shovel will work and moving it all into another adjacent space works great. This is the reason for having two or three bins side by side.
5. Anything not fully decomposed and still recognizable (such as avocado skin or pits, eggshells, etc.) should simply be tossed back onto the pile. They will all disappear in due time as the compost is formed.

I keep a gallon size plastic covered container in the kitchen for scraps as I am cooking. Once that is filled, I empty into a covered, galvanized metal garbage pail by the back door. This pail is dumped into the compost pile on a regular basis. I am always surprised at the amount of compost scraps that can be generated from one tiny kitchen by only my wife and myself: chopped up citrus fruit skins from our morning juice, egg shells, old slices of bread from the end of a loaf, small amounts of left over rice and vegetables, scraps from anything that goes into a salad, discarded artichoke leaves, potato peels, avocado skins and pits, etc. I must admit I often include seafood such as fish skin, bones, heads, shrimp shells and lobster shells. It all turns into compost.

Even apartment dwellers with very little garden space can make compost with compost appliances and devices now on the market that fit in a kitchen and function indoors. (See "sources" in the appendix).

In mid September the dogwood trees are all showing red foliage but no additional fall color are seen yet, either in the neighborhood trees or the rock garden itself. Some yellow leaves fall here and there from the weeping cherry tree but that seems to be the only sign of fall so far. The *Hymenoxis acaulis* has some late yellow flowers; the plumbago (*Ceratostigma plumbaginoides*) is still full of blue blossoms next to the geranium, which is showing only a couple of purple flowers. The *Gaura* has pink blossoms on long, thin stems but that is the extent of the rock garden color at this time.

A little weeding here and there and some deadheading is all that is really needed right now. The cooler days of approaching fall are welcome and the comfortable temperatures provide for pleasant working conditions in the garden, even though there is little necessary work.

Planted *Festuca* 'Elijah's Blue' and *Euphorbia* 'Myrsintes' in my rock garden and mulched with both a base of the ¾" stone and a full layer on top of 3/8" stone. This combination works well and stays in place beautifully.

Near the end of the month I transplanted the *Phlox* and the *Monarda* into a perennial bed elsewhere in my garden. They just became too large and out of scale for the rock garden. I mentioned these plants in the preface of this book. I loved the color and visual impact they created, especially when viewed from the house or my deck. They just were not right in the rock garden location. Any plant that outgrows its space anywhere in the rock garden should be treated in a similar manner. Fortunately I had space in another bed; otherwise, they would have ended up in the compost pile. I prepared the soil for planting additional plants in the spring. I weeded well, spread some compost and raked everything smooth. I'll add a layer of shredded leaves later in the fall and perhaps another rock or two if I can find them.

More yellow leaves are falling as September ends but still not enough to worry about at this early fall date. This is the time to trim any plants that are showing brown stems, are too "leggy" or simply spreading too aggressively. The *Gaura* is still showing pink blossoms but I cut some of the longer stems back. The *Campanula's* brown stems are also cut back now about ½ their length. Also, the oregano's long branches were cut all the way back. Later in the fall, more trimming will be required along with fall cleanup.

Any plants desired for installation this fall should be either acquired now from local nurseries or ordered through catalogs or the inter-net. This is the perfect time to plant. The days are still warm, the nights are cool without frost and generally there is some rainfall; all perfect conditions for good root growth prior to winter dormancy.

When shopping for plants, think about those that are pollinator friendly. www.pollinator.org is a good resource and they publish a free "Pollinator Friendly Planting Guide" for every zip code. They also have good plant lists for flowers that will attract birds, butterflies and insect pollinators. It is sponsored by the North American Pollinator Protection Campaign and the Pollinator Partnership. (See the "Pollinator Partnership" in "Sources").

Figure 45 Chamaecyparis obtuse 'Nana Gracilis'.

Figure 46 Rock garden in September.

Figure 47 Chamaecyparis pisifera 'Tsukumo'.

CHAPTER 10 OCTOBER

In early October I attended a program at the Mt. Cuba Center in Greenville, Delaware on "Unsung Native Rock Garden Plants". The program was conducted by Vic Piatt, their rock wall and scree garden curator for the past 17 years. Vic is one of the most knowledgeable gardeners I have met and his experience creating and maintaining the rock gardens is evident in his ability to discuss the various plants in a most informative manner.

The Mt. Cuba Center is located in rolling hills and surrounded by over 600 acres of managed natural lands. It was originally farmland, which was purchased in 1935 and developed as a private residence. Landscape architects Thomas W. Sears and Marian C. Coffin were commissioned to create a series of formal gardens and outdoor spaces that are still being maintained. Today these gardens contain over 1900 plant species native to the Appalachian Piedmont, a region of nearly 1000 miles from New Jersey to Alabama. It is located between the Atlantic Coastal Plain and the Appalachian Mountains.

The rock wall is a natural outcropping and was developed as a rock garden as the main house was being constructed in 1936. It has been maintained as what a native rock area would look like. Vic developed the scree garden across the main drive in 2007 as a continuation of the rock wall outcropping. Most of the plants are wild collected but some can be located from various sources, listed in the appendix. The native stone is known as Mt. Cuba gneiss and is different from other types of gneiss stone.

A scree develops in nature as stone tumbles down from higher elevations; Larger rocks first, then pebbles and finally dust-like particles. Vic installed most of the existing plants and many just planted themselves into the rock crevices. All of the plants are drought tolerant and all require super drainage, especially in winter.

In designing the layout of the rock garden, Vic spaces the plants in a way that color can be repeated from south to north throughout the garden. He purposefully does not over-plant. He wants the garden to look natural and in no way wants to create the look of a traditional perennial bed. His preference is to stick with species plants, rather than cultivars, sticking with wild, collected native plants. It is interesting to note that Vic does not like plant labels and feels they detract from the overall "look" of the rock garden.

Please refer to the appendix for a list of some of Mt. Cuba's specific plants, their cultural requirements and flower descriptions.

OCTOBER

In early October I planted the following plants obtained from my visit to Mt. Cuba: *Biaelowia nuttallii* (Nuttall's rayless-goldenrod), *Clinopodium georgianum* (Georgia wild basil) and *Ionactis linariifolius* (stiff aster). They each got a trowel of compost, were watered well and mulched with my crushed rock.

While driving through my neighborhood I spotted a highway expansion project where the road is being widened. The bulldozers uncovered many rocks that were strewn along the side of the road. A quick discussion with the foreman granted me permission to take a few. I chose five of a nice size and shape that I could pick up myself and loaded them into my truck. When I returned home I arranged them in the section of the rock garden where the perennials were recently removed and dug them in so that they were firm.
I still plan to mulch the area with shredded leaves later in the fall and choose
five or six more plants over the winter to install in the spring. This would be a perfect time to plant but I don't want to rush my selection decision. Perhaps some "gems" will become available in the catalogs over the winter season?

Fall cleanup should include removing all dropped leaves and stems from around rock garden plants. It is possible that this debris could harbor various fungal species that may cause powdery mildew or other diseases come next season. It is best not to compost this debris, as the pathogens on any infected tissue will not be killed, as most compost piles will not reach a high enough temperature. Should any plants appear to have diseased stems or leaves, these should be cut off at this time and discarded into trash bags for removal from the property.

Most rock garden plants are not prone to disease, especially non-woody varieties. However, should any pruning be required for infected branches or stems, cuts should be made in dry weather at least a foot below tissue showing symptoms. All pruning tools should be cleaned *between cuts* to prevent spreading any pathogens. To sanitize tools, use a bleach solution (5%), an alcohol spray or Lysol disinfectant. Disinfecting your tools is a good idea in any case throughout the summer and it should be done at the very end of the season. I buy a box of individual alcohol "wipes" sealed in plastic in the spring from any local pharmacy and keep them on hand with my tools for use throughout the year.

As the month of October passes, the change in colors of foliage becomes more and more apparent. With many of the larger oaks and maples these colors can be most dramatic, especially in the Northeast. Normally, in the rock garden, the change in leaf color is a bit more subtle but still lovely and dramatic.

These color changes result from changes in the leaf pigments, natural substances produced by the leaf cells. The most common is the green pigment, chlorophyll. The chlorophyll absorbs red and blue light from the sun so that the light reflected from the leaves looks green.

Another pigment in the leaves of most plants is carotene. Carotene absorbs blue-green and blue light. The light reflected from carotene appears yellow. During the growing season, the carotene pigment absorbs light and transfers it to the chlorophyll to assist in the process of photosynthesis. Chlorophyll and carotene are in leaf cells all through the summer. The chlorophyll covers the carotene so that summer leaves appear green, not yellow or orange. The carotene persists in leaves, even when the chlorophyll has disappeared. Once the chlorophyll disappears from the leaf, the remaining carotene causes the leaf to appear yellow, orange or brown.

Another group of pigments occurring in leaves of some plants are anthocyanins. These compounds are only produced in the fall. Anthocyanins absorb blue, blue-green and green light so the light reflected by the leaves appears red. Anthocyanins exist in cell sap and are sensitive to the sap's pH: bright red for acidic and purple for less acidic. They are formed by a reaction with sugars and certain proteins in the sap along with sunlight.

Shorter days and cooler nights trigger changes in plants. One of these changes is the growth of a membrane between branches and leaf stems that slows down the summer nutrient flow, preventing chlorophyll to be produced so that the green coloring fades. Low temperatures also destroy chlorophyll and promote the formation of anthocyanins. These anthocynanins are also enhanced by bright sunshine and dry weather. Thus, bright reds are produced in dry, sunny days followed by cool, dry nights. Not all plants can make anthocyanins. Note that red leaves occurring early in the season could be a sign of stress on the plant and not normal fall activity.

As the days become shorter, sunlight diminishes and the temperature slowly drops. Plants respond to the decreasing sunlight by producing less chlorophyll. Once the chlorophyll is no longer produced, the carotene that is also in the leaves now shows through.

The rainfall during the year will also affect the autumn leaf coloring. A dry summer can delay autumn colors and a wet fall will lower the intensity of the colors. The best combination for bright autumn colors is a warm, wet spring; a summer that's not too hot or dry and a warm, sunny fall with cool (not freezing) nights.

After mid-October, especially in the northeast, the days are mild and the nights chilly. Leaves are beginning to fall but still not enough to rake or gather. Working in the rock garden at this time consists of trimming some plants and adding more stone mulch. There are not many weeds. The thyme (*Thymus serpyllum*) is my biggest "spreader" but is easy to trim back with a pair of garden scissors (and the aroma is wonderful!).

The *Ionactis linariifolius* planted early this month is now in full bloom with lavender petals surrounding yellow centers very much like small asters.

The *Sedum sieboldii* (October daphne) is covered with pink blossoms spreading in about a two-foot radius. This is surely the plant for fall color in any rock garden.

The *Clinopodium georgianum* planted only this month is also loaded with pink blossoms and both of my *Hymenoxys* have just a few yellow flowers on long stems. The *Guara* also is blooming with pink flowers on long, drooping stems. Most of the other plants are still showing green foliage with no noticeable fall color change as yet. Many of the surrounding trees are just beginning to show their yellow, orange or red hues.

As October ends, I planted two more plants in the newly prepared section of my rock garden (definitely the last of the season). One was a back-order from a previous catalog order, *Eryngium planum* 'Jade Frost', a type of sea holly. This plant has blue green leaves with creamy white margins. The plant supposedly will have violet blue globe-like flowers with the typical spiny bracts. It is hardy to zone 5. The genus *Eryngium* is in the Apiaceae (carrot) family along with parsley, carrots celery and dill.

The other plant, *Arabis caucasica* 'Snowfix', I was able to find at a local nursery, on sale. The genus *Arabis* is in the Brassicaceae (cabbage, or mustard) family along with broccoli, cabbage and kale. It is a large genus, considered an herb but grown almost completely for ornamental purposes. The stems are usually hairy and the small flowers bloom in the spring. They love warm, sandy soil and hot, windy locations where not much else can grow. If summers are too humid, the plants can rot. My *Arabis caucasica* is also known as "wall cress", is hardy to zone 4 but excessive winter moisture can kill it.

At this time only the *Gaura* has a few pink blossoms and the *Clinopodium georgianum* is still in full pink bloom. The *Ionactis* blossoms are pretty much faded, along with the *Sedum Sieboldii* that was so brilliant all month.

The *Ceratostigma plumbagnoides* leaves are starting to turn red. The days are still mild and no other foliage is showing any fall colors. Autumn leaves are beginning to fall steadily forming a yellow, patchwork blanket over the entire rock garden.

Figure 48 Vic Piatt at Mt. Cuba rock garden.

Figure 49 Mt. Cuba scree garden.

Figure 50 Clinopodium georgianum.

Figure 51 Sedum Sieboldii (October daphne).

Figure 52 New rocks installed in October.

CHAPTER 11 NOVEMBER

This November I visited the rock garden at Temple University School of Horticulture in Ambler, Pennsylvania. It is set into a hillside bordering a main walkway and elevated to a height of about six feet. It is located in full sun most of the day.

The garden is planted heavily with mostly alpine plants cascading over the rocks. The hillside is about sixty feet long and about half is planted with Cotoneaster (C. apiculatus I think, due to the persistent red fruit) and overhangs the slope providing shade for the smaller plants underneath. There was no labeling throughout so species confirmation would be difficult. The garden is mulched with tiny stone pebbles and chips but not heavy or thick enough to resemble a scree.

The plants included lots of Thymus spp., Dianthus, Lavender, many sedums, salvia, Iberis, Euphorbias and sedge (Carex spp.). Also, tiny Iris leaves poking up here and there along with strawberry runners under the Cotoneaster.

According to the Arboretum Director, Jenny Carey, the garden is about ten years old at least, gets a severe pruning once a year and that is about it on maintenance. No fertilizer is applied. Small bulbs are added on a continual basis such as miniature daffodils, crocus and Iris providing early spring color.

The garden has the appearance of being unattended with the plants left to spread (and reseed) as they may. It is a classic example of the plants forming a living "tapestry" throughout as I have written about in preceding chapters. Overall it was very pleasant to look at and had a tranquil "feel" about it.

NOVEMBER

I don't believe in creating an artificial environment such as cold frames, fabric covering, etc. for my rock garden. I'd rather let the plants adapt (or not) to the natural conditions that surround my garden. I do utilize some devices in the vegetable garden but this seems perfectly acceptable. I suppose since growing one's food seems more utilitarian in purpose. Think of how out of place a plastic shelter would be on a high mountain path amongst true alpine plants. So, as the winter season approaches, early November brings the first frost to my rock garden. To understand the phenomenon of frost, one must first understand what is termed "dew point".

The dew point is the temperature to which a given portion of air must be cooled, at constant barometric pressure, for water vapor to condense into water. This condensed water is called "dew". The dew forms when a surface cools to a temperature that is colder than the dew point of the air next to the surface. The dew is simply the liquid water that condensed from the water vapor in the air.

The dew point and the relative humidity are closely related. The higher the humidity, the closer the dew point is to the current air temperature. At 100% relative humidity, the dew point is the same as the air temperature and the air is totally saturated with water.

Three things need to happen for frost to form:

1. The surface on which the frost forms must be *below 32 degrees Fahrenheit*. If the surface is not below 32 degrees, dew could possibly form but not frost.
2. The surrounding air must be calm with little or no wind.
3. The surface temperature must be *below* the dew point temperature. This condition guarantees that the air near the surface has more moisture than it can hold at the surface temperature. The further the surface temperature is below the dew point, the more rapidly frost will form. Note that the dew point temperature could possibly be above freezing and

frost could still form as long as the surface temperature is below freezing.

The "frost" is actually just a covering of ice crystals formed above the ground and on exposed objects when the above three conditions have been met. When frost forms on the plant's surface, no harm is actually done to the plant. It is when the water inside of the plant freezes that plant tissue is damaged.

Frost forms first at lower elevations. This fact is because cold air is denser than warm air and in calm weather cold air "pools" at ground level.

Most rock garden plants are perennials and generally become dormant after the first frosts. The entire portion of the plant above ground may turn brown and drop its leaves and flowers. The stems and dead flowers or seed heads may remain but new growth will surface when the warmer temperatures of spring arrive. Most evergreen plants will withstand the frost, although there will be no growth through the winter.

The month of November is really a pleasant time to work in the rock garden. The days are mild and there is not much to really do. Fall planting is complete, mulch is in place and most of the foliage is still green or at least, starting to show some fall coloring. There are no flowers to deadhead and no foliage to cut back. Leaves can be removed but I do not recommend raking as this action can easily disturb small seedlings and shallow roots. A leaf blower would work but I think that its use is "overkill". I prefer to hand pick the leaves, gently, around every plant. First of all, there is no hurry as winter is approaching and the leaves could actually remain in place until spring. A second reason is that you get to inspect each plant in a relaxed manner. This allows one to really see the plant's subtle changes as it prepares for winter dormancy. Southern gardeners are a bit "gypped" out of this pleasant time.

Anyone who gardens should attempt to learn the scientific (or botanical) names of their plants (genus and species). Also their classification, families, origin, name meanings and perhaps any unique characteristics.

Common names of plants leave much to be desired. They change geographically and can be called many different names throughout the United States. Language changes in other countries create a whole new set of common names that may or may not match what we have in the United States.

The process of learning the scientific (or botanical) names is a slow one and a continuous one but well worth the effort on the long run. Perhaps some record keeping strategies would help. A simple notebook is a good place to start. Any size, any shape and any style that feels comfortable and can be kept handy. A loose-leaf notebook can be started with an alphabetical listing of your own plants. This project is a bit more work but over time photos can be added, information can be updated and ultimately a nice horticultural journal results, tailor-made to your own garden.

Another method is to keep an A to Z list of genus names referring to the appropriate plant family and another list with each plant family in alphabetical order, each listing the appropriate genus. This "two-list" system is cumbersome but easily done with a computer. Without a computer it would be a nightmare.

Whatever method appeals and regardless of how long you have been gardening, a starting point can be made at any time.

Knowing the two-part genus and species name will assist you in catalog purchases, inter-net confirmation and also directly shopping in local nurseries. Every plant has this two-part name. The genus name comes first and is always capitalized. The species name is next and never capitalized. Both names are normally written in italics. The genus *Sedum* is a good example. The entire *Sedum* genus is in the Crassulaceae family, which also contains Jade plants (*Crassula argentea*) and *Sempervivum tectorum* (hen and chicks). *Sedums* come in many sizes and shapes as there are over 600 species. Most are called "stonecrops", their common name. Using the botanical name can eliminate confusion amongst the many species. For example, "English stonecrop" is actually *Sedum anglicum* (with white flowers), "shortleaf stonecrop" is *Sedum cauticola* (bright pink flowers) and "yellow stonecrop" is *Sedum reflexum* (golden yellow flowers).

Another plant exists; also called "shortleaf stonecrop" that is actually *Sedum brevifolium*. This plant has white flowers, rather than the other "shortleaf stonecrop" above (*Sedum cauticola*) that has pink flowers.

Botanical names (generally Latin or Greek) may also give a clue as to certain characteristics of a particular plant. *Lavandula* (lavender) is from the Greek *lavare* "to wash" from the Greek and Roman tradition of adding lavender to scent bath water. *Achillea* (yarrow) is named for Achilles who used the plant to heal wounds. *Salvia* (sage) is from the Latin *salvio* "I save" from various medical uses. *Thymus* (thyme) is from the Greek *thymin* "to fumigate".

Once the genus and species of a plant is confirmed, each plant within the species basically looks the same. Some may be bigger, younger, have more or less flowers, better or worse growing conditions, soil, etc., but still they pretty much look alike. Sometimes, in nature, a variation can occur that is consistent within a species. These consistent variations are called "varieties" or "subspecies" and are written with non-italics "VAR" between the species name and the variety name. For example, *Amaranthus tricolor* var. *salicifolius* is a variety of *Amaranthus* that has variegated leaves that resemble willow leaves (*salicifolius* is from *Salix*, the botanical name for "willow").

Once gardeners or growers are cultivating plants, they are no longer subjected to "nature" per se and can be propagated in such a way that a wide variety can be created within a species. A certain flower color, a dwarf growing habit, an amazing fragrance is examples of variations within the species. If these differences from the original species in nature are continued and passed along by re-seeding or asexual propagation, they are called "cultivars". The word "cultivar" is short for the words "cultivated variety". The names of these cultivars follow the species name, always start with capital letters, are never italicized and contain single quotation marks as in: *Aconitum* 'Blue Lagoon', *Aquilegia caerulea* 'Red Hobbit' and *Penstemon* 'Mystica'.

In mid November we had our first hard frost and the rock garden is showing really nice fall coloration. The *Origanum* 'Rotkugel' now has leaves of deep burgundy rather than green. The *Ceratostigma* foliage is totally red and the *Bergenia* has mostly deep maroon coloring in the leaves. The *Geranium sanguineum* now has a mixture of green and deep red leaves. The foliage of the *Euphorbia x martini* is full of its normal whorls of green leaves but the center 4 to 6 leaves of each whorl is a deep maroon. The hens and chicks are also showing a maroon tint to their leaves.

The only plants blooming at this time are the *Clinopodium georgianum* from Mt. Cuba, still with lots of pink-lavender flowers and the *Gaura* with rosy-pink-red blooms here and there on long, arching stems.

I still have more fallen leaves to clean out but they do form a lovely blanket over the white stone mulch. If the weather stays mild, snow doesn't fall and I'm not feeling lazy, I'll clean them out at my leisure. I do see some creeping wild strawberry that should be cut out at this time to prevent its sprawling throughout the garden.

The bulk of my gardening time in the past few days has been raking and shredding leaves on the rest of the property. As the rock garden gets cleaned out I'll spread some of the shredded leaves on bare spots for winter mulch; it will form compost by spring.

November passes quickly and as mentioned earlier, very little required work in the rock garden. The days remain mild with chilly nights and frost in the early morning at daybreak.
There is much work to do at this time in other parts of the garden: Weeding, mulching, turning compost piles, harvesting late fall vegetables, cutting back asparagus stalks and raspberry canes, cleaning up potager beds and adding compost for spring planting. There are still

the last fallen leaves to be raked and shredded. All the while the rock garden rests as each plant is preparing for winter dormancy.

I really love this time of year in the garden. The beds around the property look especially neat with the grounds raked clean, the beds mulched and covered with frost in the early mornings. It's time to start thinking of spring planting plans and reviewing garden notes made throughout the year. Catalogs will be coming all winter so that orders for spring delivery can be placed.

At this time photographs can be taken of the rock garden as a reminder and guide of what spaces exist, where new plants can be added and existing plants need to be relocated.

No pruning should be done at this time on any woody plants. They are preparing for dormancy and any unseasonably warm weather can stimulate fresh growth that will weaken the plant for the coming winter. Wait until the plant is fully dormant prior to pruning. In my zone 6 garden this time would be in January or February. In areas of the country where there is no freezing weather, pruning can be done at any time of the year, as required.

Figure 53 Temple Ambler's rock garden.

Figure 54 Temple Ambler's rock garden close-up.

Figure 55 November rock garden close-up.

Figure 56 November rock garden.

CHAPTER 12 DECEMBER

In mid December I was given a tour of the rock garden and surrounding area at the Henry Foundation for Botanical Research in Gladwyne, P.A. The grounds and gardens consist of 50 acres comprised of fabulous views over fields, valleys, streams and woodlands with steep slopes of giant boulders and a huge outcropping of Baltimore gneiss stone, the site of the rock garden.

The property was bought in 1927 by botanist and plant explorer Mary Gibson Henry who added adjacent farm properties through the early years resulting in the current acreage. The actual foundation was established in 1948. My tour guide was Susan Treadway, the foundation Director and also the granddaughter of Mary Henry.

In the early years of establishing the garden, hundreds of European and Asian plant species were planted on the grounds with most of the plants not surviving the harsh, Northeastern winters. This fact led Mary Henry to travel for 40 years to collect native plant species from all over the United States and Canada. In those early days it was impossible to obtain most plants from the existing trade or botanic gardens. After many years work her efforts resulted in one of the largest collections of native plants in the country.

The current rock garden, in the early 1930's, was actually not visible due to the incredible vegetative growth of honeysuckle, poison ivy, etc. covering the property. Only the very tip of the top of the stone could be seen. Once the area was cleared and the rock exposed, the planting began. Many native species of Penstemon, Phlox, Amsonia, Baptisia, Yucca, Liatris, Tradescantia, Trillium and Hamamelis were installed after the loss of the original non-native species. The surrounding areas were also planted with Styrax, 15 taxa of native Magnolias, Halesia, Rhododendron, Ilex, Viburnum and Chionanthus just to name a few.

The rock garden itself is not really planted at all with "alpine" plants but a variety of suitable natives that the massive boulders can easily accommodate. The garden is totally natural. Mary Henry was a "minimalist" according to her granddaughter, and more of a research botanist than a garden curator. There is no watering, no pesticide use or fertilizing, only planting. The plants are permitted to go to seed in winter and re-establish themselves, as they will. There is some pruning and weeding performed but only by Susan herself, not any volunteers or staff. Only she knows every plant and can identify each seedling.

It is interesting to note that in 1931, Mary Henry and her entire family spent three months mapping Northeast British Columbia. There is a mountain on the Alaskan Highway named after her, "Mt. Mary Henry". She was truly a remarkable individual up until her death in 1967.

There are many botanists on the current board of directors and they are in the process of restoring the original plants installed by Mary Henry as she left extensive, comprehensive lists and herbarium.

The Mary Henry Foundation is a "must see" for anyone interested in the native flora of America and especially for rock gardeners the world over.

DECEMBER

Normally, I do not cut back dead stems and other plant parts until almost spring. Aside from creating some winter interest I believe the plants are more prone to surviving a harsh winter if the growth is kept intact. The only mulch I use is the 3/8" and ¾" stone placed throughout the year. In some parts of the country, pine boughs can be used and other soft vegetation to assist tender plants but I leave my garden alone to fend for itself until the coming spring.

What does the term "organic gardening" actually mean today? Webster's Ninth New Collegiate Dictionary defines "organic" (in terms of gardening) as "the use of food produced with the use of feed or fertilizer of plant or animal origin without employment of chemically formulated fertilizers, growth stimulants, antibiotics or pesticides." Maria Rodale, in "Vegetables" (see bibliography) defines "organic" as "materials that are derived directly from plants or animals. Organic Gardening uses plant or animal by-products to maintain soil and plant health."

Caution is advised as the word "chemicals" is not, in it-self, organic or non-organic. Many organic substances, if not most, are indeed "chemical" by definition and are used in organic gardening practices as fertilizer, insecticides, fungicides, etc., are low in toxicity, occur naturally and basically, pose no threat to the environment if not used in excessive amounts. A better word to describe non-appropriate materials would be "synthetic" (i.e. manufactured). The intent here is the implication that "organic gardening" is a system that allows one to proceed with actions, materials, products, etc. that are not in any way harmful to the environment.

As the "organic movement" gained popularity since the 1960's, the government became involved through regulatory agencies to assure consumers that a product for use in organic practices or stated to be grown "organically" was indeed, organic. Now the fun begins!

The Federal Government, along with Trade Organizations, State Governments, private regulatory agencies and others have now published standards as to what is "organic". In 2002, under the United States Department of Agriculture (USDA), the National Organic Program (NOP) came into being and consumers started to see the "USDA Certified Organic" label on shelves in markets. The Organic Foods Production Act of 1990 mandated this organization. It consists of a member board, the National Organic Standards Board (NOSB) and is made up of farmers, food handlers, food processors, a retailer, a scientist and others. It is a marketing program within the USDA Agricultural Marketing Service (AMS). Now, products and crops can become "certified organic" by various independent agencies to guarantee their compliance with some recognized standard.

The Organic Materials Review Institute (OMRI) is now the national, nonprofit organization that determines which products are permitted to be used in organic production. OMRI listed (or approved) products may be used in operations that are "certified organic" under the NOP.

Unfortunately, there is no individual national standard and "approved" products can (and do) vary in different locations. On the good side, in most cases, the following items are now prohibited from being termed "organic":

1. Synthetic pesticides, herbicides, fungicides, genetic engineering or modification, irradiation of foods and processed sewage sludge (or biosolids) as fertilizer.

2. Livestock must be given access to pasture, they must not be given growth hormones or antibiotics and they must be given organically grown feed.

On the down side, many organic growers feel the standards as written into law are "watered-down" and they are not renewing their certification. Most large retail food outlets carry "organic" products, but they must carry the USDA organic label. Large growers are able to obtain this label by paying the certification renewal fees and obtaining required products and organisms without actually developing the sustainable ecosystem, which the smaller, original organic farmers so cherished.

In many cases, the lower food prices set by the "big business" farmers are forcing the small, truly organic growers out of business. With more organizations getting into the act, such as the Independent Organic Inspectors Association (IOIA), the "Organic Consumers' Association and others, the "organic legislation" remains in a state of flux.

So, "organic" to many people has become a legal term, defined and governed by the USDA.

Where does all this information lead to with regard to the meaning of "organic gardening" at this time?

My early indoctrination into organic gardening originated from J.I. Rodale's writings from the 1940's. He was the leading advocate against the use of what he called "chemical" fertilizers and pesticides in that they were destroying our environment. His support of using "natural" materials and processes, manure, compost and crop rotation paved the way for the organic gardening principals and practices that are gaining in popularity and support today.

I am hesitant to try and create yet another definition of the term "organic" as there is enough verbiage circulating at this time. For those that would like a bit more specific input on organic practices, the following suggestions are offered:

1. Choose the right plant for the right place. Don't try to grow something that is not suited for your particular soil or cultural accommodations. Sun, shade, soil pH, drainage and temperature all must be considered. This fact is easier said than done and will require endless experimentation. This endeavor is part of the challenge and fun of gardening.

2. Feed your soil. Constantly add organic materials such as compost, shredded leaves, dried manure, straw, sawdust, etc. and as they break down they will provide an environment for the incredible number of micro-organisms that make for a healthy soil and healthy plants.

3. Utilize diversity in your plantings. Include those plants that have scientifically proven to attract beneficial insects and pollinators and those that can potentially repel garden pests.

4. Recycle all of your organic material. Kitchen scraps, leaves, pruning debris, fallen fruit, etc. should all be composted and returned to your garden's soil.

5. Do not use synthetic pesticides, herbicides and fertilizers. They will instantly kill of beneficial insects, bacteria, and fungi and destroy the natural, healthy soil food web.

6. Do not compact your soil. Establish paths and raised beds so that there is no walking or kneeling on planted areas. The pore space in the soil must be preserved where water, air, roots and microorganisms live in harmony to support plant growth and health.

7. Do not till your soil. Roto-tilling and continual "turning over" soil causes loss of organic matter, destroys the soil structure and creates havoc with the microorganisms that provide a healthy soil food web. Add organic matter to your soil in the form of mulch.

8. Rotate your crops. Provide for at least a three-year rotation and if not possible due to space constraints, plant a cover crop for a year or two to enrich the soil.

For the gardener today, wanting to garden organically is relatively simple once removed from the governmental agencies' legal definitions. Organic gardening is still (and will always be) a system where soil fertility is maintained and replenished by utilizing organic matter, compost and mulch without the use of manufactured, synthetic chemicals. It has to do with understanding and supporting the soil food web and caring for the millions of living organisms that make up a healthy soil. In J.I. Rodale's "Encyclopedia of Organic Gardening" (see bibliography) under the section "Organic Gardening) he states: "The soil must become rich and fertile; Insect parasites and predators must be encouraged. Safe measures for control are handpicking of insect pests. Encouraging birds, interplanting with crops that repel insects, planting resistant varieties……..Good yields, truly safe food and sensible insect controls is the answer."

Over half a century later, every aspiring organic gardener is still following that advice.

My garden in December has seen severe morning frost, snow covering and over three inches of rainfall so far. The rest of the country is suffering from a major blizzard with over one foot of snow in many parts of the Midwest. Arizona actually got 20". This weather follows almost the wettest midwestern summer in history. Gardening for the year is clearly over for folks in Iowa, Illinois, Wisconsin, Nebraska, Kansas, Missouri, Michigan and most of Northern New England.

In my rock garden green foliage is still showing as winter approaches. The *Alyssum montanum* leaves are full and a very light green in color and looking great as the surrounding areas are darkened by winter's approaching dormancy. The *Sedum rupestre* is also a golden-green spreading over the rocks. Other full green foliage includes *Arabis caucasica, Veronica, Sedum reflexum, Aubrieta heterosis, Armeria* and of course the evergreens: *Picea, Chamaecyparis* and *Ilex*.

The green foliage looks especially bright in comparison to the foliage that has turned brown and the various autumn shades of dark maroon. The lavender has become a focal point with its lovely, blue-green foliage still in tact.

It is a quiet time. The garden has a subdued feeling about it as it comes to a complete rest for the winter. No attention to it is required as the year ends. In a way, the garden is representative of the year in general; reflections over various past events, projects completed or in progress and the anticipation of the New Year and all of its possibilities.

Figure 57 December rock garden.

Figure 58 Henry Foundation lower rock garden.

Figure 59 Henry Foundation upper rock garden.

"There is no end to one's continuing education. No degree is offered. One never graduates".

Sarah Stein *Planting Noah's Garden*

PLANTS THAT SHOULD NOT BE PLANTED IN A ROCK GARDEN

The plants on this list should not be planted in a normal size rock garden. By "normal size" I am considering the limit of 2500 square feet. Although this square footage is rather arbitrary, it seems to work consistently.

An exception could be a rock garden that extends through multiple environments such as a pond, a woodland setting etc. The final decision, of course, rests with each individual gardener.

1. Woody plants and shrubs, except for extreme dwarf and low growing prostrate varieties. Be especially cautious of the Junipers-if they are happy, they will spread over your other plants.

2. Aegopodium podagraria (goutweed or bishop's weed). This plant is a self-seeding nightmare for any gardener in any location. It is sold in some catalogs as "snow-on-the-mountain".

3. Houttuynia cordata. This plant is listed in many catalogs as a ground cover. Don't even think about it.

4. Lysimachia nummularia (creeping Jenny or moneywort). This plant is a prostrate perennial with trailing stems that easily root at every joint. The cultivar Lysimachia nummularia 'Aurea' has golden leaves and is less vigorous but still invasive. Take a week-end off and you're liable to find it spreading into your lawn. This plant is also listed in many catalogs as a ground cover.

5. Ornithogallum umbellatum (star of Bethlehem). Do not plant these bulbs as they will spread and take over not only your garden but your lawn.

6. Hedera helix (or any ivy cultivar). These plants are major weeds anywhere.

7. Ajuga reptans (bugleweed). Although sometimes cultivated in rock gardens due to their flowers, to me, this member of the mint family is a spreading weed and best not planted at all.

8. Opuntia humifusa (prickly pear). Although a native with profuse yellow flowers from spring to summer, watch out! This plant creeps along the ground, has sharp spines and is almost impossible to "clean-up" in spring and is difficult to mulch. Also, there are small, sharp hairs on the surface of its joints which you will find under your skin without fail!

9. Cotoneaster. Includes many species that creep and spread, including some deciduous, some evergreen and some semi-evergreen. They need a great deal of space and most are too large for a small, confined rock garden. Most have persistent red fruit and many have brilliant leaf coloring in autumn. They are also prone to certain diseases and insects in dry summers such as fire blight, lace bugs and spider mites. In the organic garden without resorting to chemical sprays, this genus should not be planted.

10. Vinca (periwinkle) both Vinca minor and Vinca major. These plants will absolutely take over, rambling over everything, especially with some shade.

11. Pachysandra. Pachysandra procumbens (Allegheny spurge) is a North American native and Pachysandra terminalis (Japanese spurge) is the Asian native so often used as a shady ground cover. Forget about planting either one in your rock garden.

12. Vines or climbers of any type.

13. Tall perennial or annual grasses. Many small grasses are perfectly suitable for the rock garden, however, be cautious of anything tall and spreading. Some examples of totally out of

scale and inappropriate plants would include: Arundo domax (giant reed), Miscanthus spp., Spartina pectinata, Stipa gigantea, Erianthus ravennae, Cyperus papyrus, Panicum spp., Calamagrostis acutiflora stricta and Cortaderia selloana just to name a few.

14. Bamboo of any kind.

15. Be careful of ferns. Some are small and look great amongst the rocks and in small crevices but many are too big, spread too much and look out of place, especially in a sunny rock garden. Do your homework!

16. Bog plants requiring a continuously moist soil.

17. All annuals. For the most part, these popular summer bloomers will detract from the subtle blossoms and foliage of your alpine and sub-alpine collection of rock garden plants. Forget about petunias, impatiens, zinnias and the like.

18. Standard size spring bulbs such as daffodils, tulips, hyacinth, etc. Their scale is too large and requires the leaves to remain until the end of June in most cases until they turn yellow & brown. They will surely overshadow the smaller, tender, spring flowering rock garden perennials. Small crocus may be fine and some dwarf, native tulips (there are many). Galanthus (snowdrops) and Scilla are fine. The dwarf daffodils also can work, such as Narcissus minimus. There are many others, so dilligence is required in seeking them out.

19. Traditional tall and spreading perennial plants found in typical beds and borders throughout the country. Some popular examples would include the following list. Again, the complete list is long (and possibly endless, due to new cultivars every year):

Ahemilla (lady's-mantle)
Antirrhinum (snapdragons)
Astilbe
Baptisia (wild or false indigo)
Boltonia
Centranthus (red valerian)
Delphinium
Dicentra (bleeding heart)
Digitalis (foxglove)
Helianthus (sunflower)
Hemerocallis (daylily)
Hosta
Paeonia (peony)
Rudbeckia (coneflower)
Scabiosa (pincushion)
Solidago (goldenrod)
Tradescantia

20. Asarum. Woodland plants, called wild ginger, which need plenty of moisture and spread. Better planted in a woodland garden than in a rock garden.

21. Orchids, even terrestrial natives. Soil and moisture needs are far too specialized to be considered for a rock garden.

22. Euonymus fortunei (wintercreeper). A ground cover which will smother your entire garden.

23. Roses of any type (even the "cute" little miniatures).

24. Heuchera (coral bells). These plants belong in the woods, not the rock garden.

25. Helleborus (christmas roses). These plants, as wonderful as they are, belong under trees that lose their leaves in winter, especially in woodland gardens.

26. Mints of any kind (Mentha spp.). In a short time they will take over your entire rock garden.

27. Verbascum (mulleins). Great flowers, too tall, large floppy leaves, not what you want in your rock garden.

MY ROCK GARDEN PLANTS

All plants listed require excellent drainage. Sources for information include catalogs, guidebooks, encyclopedias, bibliography references, the Internet and my own experience and observations. Quotation marks signify a direct quote from the listed, named catalog.

NAME	DATE PLANTED	SOURCE	LIGHT	ZONE
Achillea 'Moonshine'	4/14/08	High Country Gardens	Full sun	3-9

"…..highly adaptable in its soil and water needs. The distinctive silver-gray foliage is a fine backdrop for the lemon-yellow flower clusters that keep coming all summer."

Aconitum 'Blue Lagoon'	4/14/08	Wayside Gardens	Part shade	4-8

" A compact cultivar ideal for containers, this exceptionally heavy bloomer sets buds lower on the stems, for a brighter, more floriferous display. The hooded blue blooms stand out in late season, when other blue-flowered perennials have passed……."

Agastache 'Acapulco Salmon & Pink'	4/14/08	High Country Gardens	Full sun	5-10

"A wonderful hybrid introduction to be enjoyed for its mint-scented foliage and a profusion of bi-colored orange and pink tubular flowers. A continuous bloomer, 'Acapulco Salmon & Pink' is in color all summer……." Propagate by seed, cuttings or root division. Most agastache will re-seed readily.

Alyssum montanum 'Mountain Gold'	7/13/09	Albrecht's Nurseries	Full sun	3-8

"Masses of fragrant gold flowers April to May. Fine foliage and a low habit".

Anthemis tinctoria 'Susanna Mitchell'	4/14/08	High Country Gardens	Full sun	3-8

"……lights up the garden with a non-stop display of creamy-white daisies most of the summer. A vigorous, easily grown plant, it has finely textured foliage and lax, mounding stems. Best grown in infertile, well drained soil without much supplemental irrigation. Pinch or shear stem tips in mid-spring to thicken up the plants….."

Aquilegia caerulea 'Red Hobbit'	4/14/09	High Country Gardens	Partial to full shade	4-8

Red Hobbit columbine. "…..a dwarf selection with red and white flowers. It likes compost enriched soil with regular irrigation and afternoon shade. This stable hybrid comes true to color when reseeding in the garden."

Arabis caucasica 'Snow Fix' (rock cress)	5/20/09	Albrecht's Nurseries	Full sun	4-8

"A reliable solution for hot, windy locations where nothing else can grow. Compact mounds of colorful, dainty flowers. Charming when tucked into rock crevices or walls.

NAME	DATE PLANTED	SOURCE	LIGHT	ZONE
Arctostaphylos			Sun to partial shade	4

Heath family (ericaceae); About 50 species of evergreen, woody plants, many of a prostrate form. They generally have small flowers and red fruit. They like sandy or rocky acid soil in either full sun or partial shade. Propagated by top cuttings or in creeping species by transplanting seed.

NAME	DATE PLANTED	SOURCE	LIGHT	ZONE
Arctostaphylos coloradoensis	4/14/08	High Country Gardens	Partial sun	5-8

Hybrid manzanita. "This fantastic hybrid groundcover shrub was originally found growing on the high, cold Uncompaghre Plateau of western Colorado. The plant is a robust evergreen shrub with cinnamon-red exfoliating bark, shell-pink flowers in spring, and red fruit in the fall. Plant in morning sun areas, in a well-drained soil. Keep regularly watered for the first few growing seasons to establish itself."

NAME	DATE PLANTED	SOURCE	LIGHT	ZONE
Armeria maritima 'Pink Lusitanica'	5/12/08	Albrecht's Nursery	Full sun	4-8

Wide natural distribution in the United States and Europe. Low growing perennial with dense tufts of grass-like foliage topped by pink, pom-pom-like flowers in spring. A virtually carefree plant that tolerates most soils in full sun. Insect and disease resistant.

NAME	DATE PLANTED	SOURCE	LIGHT	ZONE
Artemesia versicolor 'Seafoam'	4/14/08	High Country Gardens	Full sun	4-10

Curlicue sage. "The foamy curls of this fragrant sage create a soft mat of gray........"

NAME	DATE PLANTED	SOURCE	LIGHT	ZONE
Aubrieta heterosis 'Novalis Blue'	5/11/09	Albrecht's Nurseries	Full sun or partial shade	

Purple rockcress. Pale blue flowers larger than other varieties.

NAME	DATE PLANTED	SOURCE	LIGHT	ZONE
Bergenia 'Bressingham Ruby'	7/25/08	Albrecht's Nursery	Full sun or partial shade	3-8

Saxifrage family (Saxifragaceae). Asiatic perennial with about 12 species. They have small, pink flowers and are prey to slugs. This is Bergenia cordifolia. Can be grown as a stand-alone plant but does well as it spreads to an evergreen ground cover. Foliage is pest free, thick and leathery. Early deep, rosy red flowers in spring are an added treat to a plant that yields amazing foliage 12 months a year. Prefers humus-enriched soil. Increase by division of established clumps. Handsome evergreen foliage turns ruby bronze in cool weather and new growth in spring emerges green.

NAME	DATE PLANTED	SOURCE	LIGHT	ZONE
Biaelowia nuttallii	10/1/09	Mt. Cuba Center	Full sun	

Nutall's rayless-goldenrod.

NAME	DATE PLANTED	SOURCE	LIGHT	ZONE
Calylophus serrulatus	4/14/08	High Country Gardens	Full sun	4-9

Dwarf sundrops. "A little known native from the short grass prairies of the western Great Plains. But not for long! It is a heavy-bloomer from late spring through the summer. This tough plant will be the star of your xeriscape. Dwarf sundrops likes a lean, well-drained soil and a good shearing before the growing season starts in late spring to keep it looking tidy and loaded with flowers."

NAME	DATE PLANTED	SOURCE	LIGHT	ZONE

Campanula rotundifolia   4/14/08   High Country Gardens   Full sun to partial shade   3-9

Bluebell of Scotland. "Wiry stems of nodding blue flowers grace this native wildflower. Blooms continuously from early summer on. This little charmer blends well into any perennial border. Campanula grow best in good garden soils with watering. A very cold hardy perennial......" Dies back to the ground each winter, but brown stems are persistent if not pruned in fall.

Caryopteris x clandonensis 'Longwood Blue'   3/27/08   High Country Gardens   Full sun to partial shade   5-9

"Blue mist shrub" is the common name. "Selected at Longwood Gardens of Pennsylvania for its upright growth, long bloomtime, heavy flower production, and superb silvery foliage......
...The blooms are sky-blue, standing out against highly aromatic foliage...."

Ceratostigma plumbaginoides   4/14/08   High Country Gardens   Full sun to partial shade   5-9

"Hardy plumbago" or "leadwort" is the common name. "An outstanding, long-lived groundcover that slowly weaves itself into the garden fabric, creating large drifts of fall color. The deep-blue flowers are numerous and long lasting beginning in early fall. As the flowering finishes, the leaves begin a month-long change to a vivid mahogany red color. Plumbago is extremely adaptable, growing equally well in sun or shade and thriving in a wide range of soil types." Native to China and Africa. Great ground cover, bearing true blue flowers whether in sun or shade to 12" tall. Pest free, with brilliant red fall color as cooler temperatures set in. Propagate by spring division or cuttings. Late to emerge in spring so care should be taken around dormant plants (another good reason for the use of labels).

Chamaecyparis obtusa 'Nana Gracilis'   10/1/09   Albrecht's Nurseries   Full sun   5

Dwarf green Hinoki Cypress. "The most sold dwarf Japanese Hinoki on the market. Dark green leaves that look like cupped eye-lids. Makes a conical plant that looks good in any rock garden. Very tight foliage. At 50 years old 12 feet tall. Height x spread in 10 years 3 ft. x 2 ft.."

Chamaecyparis pisifera 'Tsukumo'   10/1/09   Albrecht's Nurseries   Full sun   5

"A miniature, flat, bun-shaped Swara Cypress. Leaves green, curly and thick. This could be a "refind" of an old Japanese cultivar. Plant grows 1 inch a year. Found by Spingarn about 1967.Height x spread in 10 years: 3 in. x 1 ft.".

Clinopodium georgianum   10/1/09   Mt. Cuba Center   Full sun   6
   Georgia wild basil.

Convalaria majalis 'Rosea'   4/24/08   Park Seed Company   Shade   4

"Lily-of-the-valley" in the lily family (liliaceae). Not an American native. Bell shaped, very fragrant flowers (normally white but 'Rosea' has pink flowers. 6-12" tall blooming in late spring. Soil should be enriched annually with organic matter. Propagate by division. Thin plantings when flowering becomes sparse.

NAME	DATE PLANTED	SOURCE	LIGHT	ZONE
Dianthus gratianapolitanus 'Firewitch'	4/14/08	High Country Gardens	Full sun to partial shade	3-9

"Cheddar pink" is common name, of Eurasian descent. Leaves form a gray-green grassy mat. Grows in ordinary garden soil and does well if dry. Remove spent flower stalks for tidiness. 6-8" in height. Increase by seeds, cuttings or division. "2005 Perennial Plant of the Year. 'Firewitch' is superb for both its bright gray-blue foliage and its bouquet fragrant hot-pink flowers in late spring. More xeric than many Dianthus, "firewitch" likes a lean, well drained soil with plenty of sunshine.

NAME	DATE PLANTED	SOURCE	LIGHT	ZONE
Digitalis obscura	4/20/08	High Country Gardens	Full to partial sun	5-9

"Narrow leaf foxglove" is the common name. "2004 Plant Select Winner. A rugged perennial species from the mountains of Spain, late spring blooming Digitalis obscura is very different from the woodland foxgloves commonly offered. The brown and yellow bell-like flowers are extremely attractive; the upright woody stems and evergreen lily-like leaves are also very ornamental. Plant Digitalis obscura in full or partial sun in lean-to-average garden soils."

NAME	DATE PLANTED	SOURCE	LIGHT	ZONE
Eryngium planum 'Paradise Jackpot'	4/24/08	Wayside Gardens	Full sun to partial shade	5-8

"Masses of spiky violet-blue blooms arise on this drought-tolerant, deer-resistant little plant!...... .....these 1/4- to 1/2-inch blooms are surrounded by layers of pointed bracts of brilliant blue. Distinctive and utterly carefree!"

NAME	DATE PLANTED	SOURCE	LIGHT	ZONE
Euphorbia x martini	4/26/08	Albrecht's Nursery	Full sun to part shade	5-7

"Martin's spurge" is a really pretty Euphorbia, a cross between E. characias and E. amagdaloids Rubra' and forms an evergreen clump of leathery, gray-green foliage, both the stems and new growth being flushed with a burgundy color. Lime-green flowers appear in June through early summer.

NAME	DATE PLANTED	SOURCE	LIGHT	ZONE
Euphorbia myrsinites	9/1/09	Wayside Gardens	Full sun	5-9

"A generous perennial always ready to tackle poor dry soils, excessive heat, and punishing drought, myrtle spurge is the focal point of many a fine rock garden and driveway planting. Its cool blue-gray foliage spirals upward around each stiff stem, crowned with sulfur-yellow blooms. Deadhead promptly to avoid the plant self-sowing, or let it multiply gloriously in the sun-soaked garden."

NAME	DATE PLANTED	SOURCE	LIGHT	ZONE
Festuca ovina 'Elijah Blue'	9/1/09	Wayside Gardens	Full sun to partial shade	4-8

"Sturdy, compact habit for decorative groundcover, accent, edging, rock gardens. Height: 10" x Width: 12" ".

NAME	DATE PLANTED	SOURCE	LIGHT	ZONE
Gaura lindheimeri 'Crimson Butterflies'	3/27/08	Wayside Gardens	Full sun to partial shade	3-8

"Hot pink blooms on compact bright red 8 to 10-inch stems from spring through fall. The hotter the summer the redder the foliage!"

NAME	DATE PLANTED	SOURCE	LIGHT	ZONE
Genista			Full sun	6

Pea family (Leguminosae). Evergreen, flowers pea-like, yellow or white. Fruit is a longish, flattened pod. Does not transplant easily. Increase by seeds or layering.

Genista lydia	4/24/08	High Country Gardens		

"Woadwaxen" or "broom", Native to Europe. They make stemmy mounds and cover themselves with yellow, pea-shaped flowers. Ordinary garden soil is fine, they are not "picky" but are difficult to transplant once established. "The profuse yellow flowers of Genista lydia completely smother the plant, making this small shrub a highlight in the spring garden. The plant has cascading evergreen stems that drape gracefully over ledges. G. lydia is a slow but steady grower, eventually forming an impressive groundcover-like shrub. Nice for use on hot, sunny slopes when planted close together on 18" centers...."

Geranium sanguineum 'Max Frei'	7/1/08	Albrecht's Nursery	Full sun	4

"Blood-red cranesbill" in the geranium family (Geraniaceae). Low, prostrate with red flowers in early spring. It likes rich soil and can be increased by division of clumps in spring or fall or grown from seed. Tolerates full sun, even in hot, dry summers.

Hymenoxys

Rocky mountain native. Yellow, daisy-like flower. There are many forms as it grows at many varying elevations.

Hymenoxys Hymenoxys acaulis 'Sundancer Daisy'	4/24/08	High Country Gardens	Full sun	5-10

"Attractive thread-leaf foliage covered by daisies from late spring through fall."

Hymenoxys scaposa	4/24/08	High Country Gardens	Full sun	4-9

"Thrift-leaf Perky Sue" is the common name. "A wonderful everblooming yellow daisy that is both heat-loving and drought tolerant. The foliage is evergreen and looks just like Armeria. A vigorous re-seeder, it quickly colonizes harsh areas of the garden. Perky Sue loves gravel mulch....."

Iberis sempervirens 'Little Gem'	4/20/08	High Country Gardens	Full sun	5

A perennial herb from the Mediterranean region, formally the mustard family (Cruciferae) but now in the cabbage family (Brassicaceae). "Candytuft" is the common name. Will stop flowering if too dry. Cut back after flowering (spring to summer) to maintain compact growth. Grows to about 12" tall. May require a light mulch to keep foliage from browning. It remains evergreen throughout the year.
".....a wonderful dwarf form of common Candytuft, sharing its larger relative's handsome evergreen foliage and large white flower clusters. Very effective mixed with other rock garden species...."

Ilex x 'Rock Garden'	5/2/09	Albrecht's Nursery	Full sun	3-8

A miniature form of Holly. New hybrid developed by Rutgers University. Leaves dark green on a flat, round spreading bun. Red berries in winter time but very sparse. Height to only 4" in ten years with a 14" spread.

NAME	DATE PLANTED	SOURCE	LIGHT	ZONE
Imperata cylindrical rubra 'Red Baron'	7/1/08	Albrecht's Nursery	Sun to light shade	5-9

"Japanese blood grass", to 12" high in the grass family (Gramineae). Ornamental grass introduced into the United States from Japan. Leaves are deep red but green at the base. Reasonably fertile, moist soil is best. Increase by division. Water weekly during dry spells and remove any pure green shoots as they appear. NOTE: Considered invasive in Florida, Georgia and Virginia.

Ionactis linariifolius Stiff aster.	10/1/09	Mt. Cuba Center	Full sun	6

Lavandula angustifolia 'Nana'	4/24/08	High Country Gardens	Full sun	5-10

Native to Southern Europe and North Africa, evergreen with a well-known fragrance to both flowers and foliage. Shear back plants after flowering or in early spring to keep them from becoming leggy. ".......The thin, blue flower spikes are held above the attractive blue-gray leaves on short, stiff stems. Lavandula angustifolia 'Nana' grows slowly to form very dense, 6" high, flattened mounds of fragrant foliage. Reports from the Denver area indicate that it's an exceptionally cold-hardy cultivar."

Lewisia cotyledon 'Sunset Strain'	4/24/08	High Country Gardens	Partial shade	5

A North American native in many colors. Soil must be very well drained, a bit of shade and soil should be on the acid side. Try various locations throughout your garden until the plant thrives in the right spot. Showy flower clusters in many, many pastel shades.

Oenothera 'Blushing Rosie'	9/20/06	Spring Hill Nursery	Full sun	5

"Sundrops" is the common name (Oenothera tetragona). It grows to about 18" tall and tolerates dry soil. It is the evening primrose family (Onagraceae) and these plants are native to the western United States. They normally have yellow flowers in summer and can be increased by division.
"Oenothera 'Blushing Rosie' produces loads of deep rose-pink flowers with yellow stamens for many weeks throughout the summer. Foliage turns gray green to scarlet to burgundy as cold weather approaches....."

Origanum 'Rotkugel'	4/24/08	High Country Gardens	Full sun to partial shade	5-9

"Introduced into the U.S. by Dan Hinkley, this is an improvement on older cultivars. 'Rotkugel' is floriferous and has a mounding habit in flower. The plant forms low-spreading mats of foliage that come into bloom from August through October. The flowering stems have large, loose heads of bi-colored flowers with dark purple calyces and deep pink flowers. Butterflies love this plant."

Pelargonium endlicherianum	4/14/08	High Country Gardens	Full sun to partial shade	4-8

"Turkish geranium" is the common name. "An incredible wildflower from the Taurus mountains of southwestern Turkey. Turkish Pelargonium is a perennial gem that will dazzle you with its large bright pink flowers in early summer. Closely related to the common garden geranium this very cold hardy plant forms a tidy mound of round, crinkled dark green leaves and grows easily in infertile, well-drained soil. Although xeric, don't grow it too dry; deep watering every week to ten days when there is no rain keeps established plants happy. In hotter, non-mountain areas, plant in partial shade."

NAME	DATE PLANTED	SOURCE	LIGHT	ZONE
Penstemon 'Blue Midnight'	4/20/08	High Country Gardens	Full sun	6-9

"A hybrid variety with outstanding parentage. 'Blue Midnight' is a cross between one of my all-time favorite garden performers, P. strictus and the showy Mexican species P. gloxinioides. The resulting plant is a vigorous grower with substantial green foliage and large, plump eye-catching flowers for much of the summer. The individual flowers are bluish-purple in color with showy mulberry streaks in the throat….."

Penstemon x mexicale 'Red Rocks'	4/29/08	Park Seed Company	Sun to part shade	5-9

"From late spring until the end of fall, this tireless bloomer covers itself in brilliant magenta-and-white flowers! The foliage is evergreen and the habit very compact on this super-vigorous award winner. Drought-tolerant, it flowers best if cut back after the first blooms pass."

Penstemon 'Mystica'	4/20/08	Park Seed Company	Full sun	4-8

"This heavy-blooming native perennial has it all - light lavender-pink blooms that crowd along sturdy charcoal-black stems over a long, long season, followed by autumn foliage of rich bronzy-red. Great for cutting, these flowers bring butterflies and hummingbirds flocking, stand up to severe heat and humidity, and need almost no attention from you. What could be better in the sunny garden?

Penstemon pinifolius 'Nearly Red'	4/24/08	High Country Gardens	Full sun to Partial shade	4-9

"I was thrilled when I came across this distictive form some years ago. With its long, graceful, nearly red tubular flowers, it really stood out among its orange flowered neighbors. 'Nearly Red' also has nice evergreen, needle-like foliage. Summer blooming……."

Phlox subulata 'Blue Emerald'	3/19/09	Lowes	Full sun	6

Blue Emerald creeping phlox. Blue flowers in early spring.

Phlox subulata 'Fort Hill'	3/19/09	Lowes	Full sun	6

Fort Hill creeping phlox. Pink flowers in early spring.

Picea abies 'Little Gem'	3/27/08	Wayside Gardens	Full sun to Partial shade	2

North American native, evergreen with sharp, pointed needles. They like moist soil enriched with organic matter….. "this diminutive beauty retains its very dwarf, dense habit. Naturally rounded, it needs no pruning. Best in cool climates. Ultimately reaching a height of only 1 foot with similar spread."

Salvia pachyphylla 'Blue Flame'	4/20/08	High Country Gardens	Full sun	5-9

"……..a selection of the xeric sub-shrub Giant Purple Sage, chosen for its huge, brightly colored 10" plus long flowering spikes. Like a gas flame, the long tubular blue flowers poke through the rose-pink bracts attracting hummingbirds from the entire neighborhood. To help support the huge flower spikes, it's helpful to pinch back the tips of the new shoots in mid-spring to thicken up the plant. This beauty likes full sun, good air circulation and fast draining soil conditions."

NAME	DATE PLANTED	SOURCE	LIGHT	ZONE
Santolina chaecyparissus	4/20/08	High Country Gardens	Full sun	5-10

"Lavender cotton", 1-2' tall and blooms in summer. Likes dry soil. Aster family (Asteraceae) which used to be called the daisy family (Compositae). Evergreen, aromatic, mainly from the Mediterranean region. Lovely, small, globe-shaped yellow flowerheads and aromatic silver-gray foliage. Grows best in sandy or loam soil and it will not do well in clay. Propagate by summer stem cuttings, which root easily in sand. Prune after flowering to prevent plants from becoming ragged. Should be mulched where winters are cold.

Saponaria ocymoides	4/20/08	Miller Nurseries	Full sun	4

Native to the mountains of southern Europe. "Soapwort", its common name, forms a loose mat of dark green foliage with lavender-pink flowers in summer. Remains evergreen throughout the year.

Saxifraga arendsii 'Purple Robe'	10/27/08	Colibraro Nurseries	Partial sun to partial shade	5-7

Delicate stems bear a profusion of tiny, crimson flowers in mid spring above a cushiony mat of extremely compact, mossy green foliage. Spent flowers should be removed for a neater appearance.

Sedum dasyphyllum 'Major'	4/28/08	Albrecht's Nursery	Full sun to partial shade	4

Native to Europe and North Africa, this is a perennial forming a low mat of ovoid gray-blue leaves and white flowers flushed with pink.

Sedum hispanicum	6/11/09	Robert Seit	Full sun	6
Sedum reflexum 'Blue Spruce'	7/13/09	Albrecht's Nurseries	Full sun	4-7

Stonecrop. "One of the least demanding, most satisfying perennials in the garden. Attracts butterflies. Classic plants for rock gardens".

Sedum sexangulare	5/11/09	Albrecht's Nursey	Full sun	3-9

Watch chain stonecrop. "Low growing with jellybean-like foliage that turns shades of rose and copper with yellow flowers in summer".

Sedum sieboldii	8/4/08	Albrecht's Nursery	Full sun to partial shade	3-9

Native to Japan, forming a slowly spreading clump of gray leaves with rose-pink flowers late in the summer to fall. This plant is especially attractive to slugs. Ordinary to poor soil is fine and doesn't need excessive watering. Common name is "October Daphne stonecrop".

Sedum spurium 'Dragon's Blood'	5/2/09	Albrecht's Nursery	Full sun to partial shade	3-9

"Stonecrop" blooms from early summer to fall with vibrant red flowers. Easy to maintain and thrives in hot, dry locations.

NAME	DATE PLANTED	SOURCE	LIGHT	ZONE
Sedum spurium 'John Creech'	7/13/09	Albrecht's Nurseries	Full sun to partial shade	3-9

Pink to red blooms mid to late summer.

Sedum spurium 'Tricolor'	7/13/09	Albrecht's Nurseries	Full sun	4-9
Sempervivum tectorum hardy species mix	4/28/08	Albrecht's Nursery	Full sun to partial shade	4-5

Native to Europe and North Africa, are evergreen and come in a huge selection of sizes, shapes and colors. Divide and replant young rosettes in spring or summer when they appear very crowded. They do well in the worst soil and can be dried out considerably.

Sempervivum tectorum 'Red Beauty'		4/28/08	Albrecht's Nursery	

See also notes for S. tectorum above.

Silene 'Robert Seit'	6/11/09	Robert Seit	Full sun	6
Teucrium			Full sun	5-6

Germander, in the mint family (Labiatae). Grows in average to poor soil. Drought tolerant once established. Prune winter-damaged top growth in early spring. Propagate by division or summer cuttings.

Teucrium aroanium	4/24/08	High Country Gardens	Full sun to partial shade	5-10

"......Gray creeping germander grows into a low mound of thin, silver leaves that form a beautiful backdrop for the honey-scented, deep lavender-pink flowers. Shear back by 1/3 in mid-spring to re-invigorate established plants. Plant in lean, well-drained soils and mulch with gravel for best performance.

Thymus serpyllum 'Ruby Glow'	4/16/09	Wayside Gardens	Full sun	4

"Creeping thyme" or "mother-of-thyme". Grows to about 4" tall in average garden soil, not too rich. Creeping, mat-forming, woody at the base with red flowers that are attractive to bees. There are many different color forms. Can be increased by cuttings or division. Planted mine at top of sculpture.

Verbena peruviana 'Red'	5/14/08	High Country Gardens	Full sun	6-10

"Vervain" in the verbena family (Verbenaceae). Native to North and South America. There are about 200 species. This is supposedly one of the most cold hardy of the Verbena.The brilliant red flowers bloomed all summer. Propagate by seeds in early spring or cuttings taken in the fall. Prune in fall to promote dense growth. I should have mulched it in fall but I didn't.

NAME	DATE PLANTED	SOURCE	LIGHT	ZONE
Veronica 'New Century'	5/20/09	Albrecht's Nurseries	Full sun to partial shade	2-8

Speedwell. "This excellent, new flowering groundcover lierally covers itself in small blue flowers in late April-May. The evergreen foliage is wonderfully thick and deep green".

Zauschneria california 'Waynes Select'	4/24/08	High Country Gardens	Full sun	5-9

"Of our many native western wildflowers, Zauschneria is one of the best sources of "natural nectar". Wayne's Select' extends the hummingbird attracting season by blooming in early fall with dusky scarlet trumpets. Especially valued for its very showy silver foliage, this is a slow-to-spread variety that works well in smaller spaces....."

Mt. Cuba Center Plants of interest in the rock wall and scree gardens

Please note that winter drainage is the most important cultural factor on all of these plants. "Wet feet" will cause them all to disappear. Also, no fertilization is required.

Bigelowia nuttallii
Nuttall's rayless-goldenrod
- Aster family
- Perennial evergreen tuft of grassy foliage
- Wirey flower stem terminates in a candelabra-like arrangement of golden yellow ray-less flowers
- Late summer into autumn blooming
- Very draught tolerant, growing in rocky, granitic sites
- Full sun, thin sandy to gravely soils
- Seeds in well where happy

Ipomopsis rubra
Standing cypress
- Phlox family
- Biennial 2' to 4' tall
- Finely dissected, feathery foliage
- Tap rooting, drought tolerant
- Showy red tubular flowers, dotted red and yellow in throat
- Blooms June through September
- Attracts hummingbirds
- Full sun, medium to dry soil
- Seeds in well where happy

Liatris pilosa
Shaggy gayfeather

- Aster family
- Perennial, but treated as an annual as it seeds in heavily
- Erect, narrow spike to 3' tall
- Linear, narrow grass-like foliage along stem
- Violet to purple flowers – 9 to 12 per head
- Blooms from the tip down
- Blooms from late summer into autumn
- Attracts butterflies
- Full sun

Phemeranthus teretifolius
Appalachian rock-pink

- Portulaca family
- Annual or perennial (seeds heavily)
- 3" to 8" tall basal foliage, 1" wirey flower scape
- Foliage is cylindrical in cross section, 1" to 2" long and designed for water storage
- Vibrant rose-purple flowers, ½" wide in loose cluster, open late afternoon
- Blooms June through October
- Full sun

Symphyotrichum (Aster) ericoides v. prostratum 'Snow Flurry'
Snow Flurry white heath aster

- Aster family
- Perennial, herbaceous to woody, 4" to 6" tall with rigid sprawling stems
- Leaves roughly 1" long by 1'4" wide, linear and stiff
- Flowers are white with yellow center, ½" wide and star-shaped
- Blooms late summer into autumn and cover the plant at peak bloom

- Full sun best, tolerant of light shade, drought tolerant
- Cut all the way back in late fall or early winter

Ionactis linariifolius
Stiff aster

- Aster family
- Perennial, herbaceous to woody, 6" to 20" tall
- Foliage is linear and narrow, needle-like and stiff, ¾" to 2" long by 1/8" wide
- Flowers are shades of lavender-blue sometimes white, golden yellow disc that ages to red-orange, ¾" to 1" wide
- Blooms September through October
- Full sun best, but will take some shade

Helianthus porteri
Confederate daisy

- Aster family
- Annual, herbaceous, 1' to 2' tall with equal spread, seeds in prolifically
- Leaves 3" to 4" long by ½" wide, medium to dark green, lanceolate
- Flowers are golden yellow, 1" wide
- Blooms September into November
- Full sun best, will tolerate shade but tends to flop

Silene virginica
Fire pink

- Dianthus family
- Perennial, short lived, herbaceous, clump forming, 10" to 15" tall
- Foliage is pale to deep green, leathery, 3" to 6" long by 1" to 1-1/4" wide
- Flowers are sticky, five-petaled, each petal deeply notched at the tip, brilliant red, displayed in loose clusters on sticky stems

- Blooms spring to autumn and attracts hummingbirds
- Usually found in part shade in moist well drained soil but does well in full sun

Sedum ternatum
Three-leaf stonecrop

- Stonecrop family
- Perennial, herbaceous, 3" to 6" tall and creeping
- Foliage is evergreen, succulent, designed for water storage as are the stems
- Flowers are four pointed, white star-shaped, ½" wide, held above foliage
- Blooms April through June
- Part shade best but does well in full sun

Phlox subulata
Moss phlox

- Phlox family
- Perennial, herbaceous evergreen ground cover, 3" to 6" tall and spreading to 2'
- Leaves are medium to dark green, awl-like, ½" to 1" long, prickly to the touch
- Flowers are fragrant, ¾" five-petaled with each petal notched at the tip, vibrant shades of pink, red, lavender, blue-purple or white
- Best in full sun though tolerant of some shade

Eurybia hemispherica
Prairie wood aster

- Aster family
- Perennial, herbaceous to woody, 2' tall
- Leaves linear and narrow, stiff and rough to the touch 4-1/2" long by ¼" wide

- Flowers are 1-1/2" wide, medium to dark violet-blue, bright yellow center that ages to a reddish-brown
- Best in full sun but tolerant of some shade

A GENERAL LIST OF SOME ROCK GARDEN PLANTS

All plants listed require excellent drainage. Sources for information include catalogs, guidebooks, encyclopedias, bibliography references, the Internet and my own experience and observations.

NAME	COMMON NAME	LIGHT REQUIRED	ZONE
Achillea ageratifolia	Greek Yarrow	Full sun	4-8

Mat-like evergreen foliage covered with clusters of small white daisies in late spring.

Achillea tomentosa 'Maynard's Gold'	Wooly Yarrow	Full sun	3

A perennial in the aster or sunflower family (Asteraceae) which used to be called the daisy family (Compositae), growing to 8" high. Ordinary garden soil is fine. Native to Europe & northern Asia. Bright yellow flowers in spring. Many cultivars are available. Propagate by seed or by dividing roots in the spring or fall. Soil can be of poor to moderate fertility.

Adiantum pedatum	hardy maidenhair fern or five-finger fern	Partial sun & partial shade	1-8

A distinct North American species, growing from sub-artic North America to the southern U.S. Prefers humus-rich soil and will grow around rocks and on vertical rock walls but requires moisture. Pteridaceae, or maidenhair fern family. Grows to a bit over one foot in height, perennial and a
slow spreader

Aethionema grandiflorum	Persian stone cress	Full sun	6

Native to Lebanan & Iran. This is a pink flower, related to Iberis (candytuft). It's beautiful, deep blue-green foliage is attractive all year long. Drought tolerant and needs to be sheared lightly after flowering.

Allium schubertii	ornamental onion or Schubert onion	Full sun to partial shade	3-9

Alliaceae family, blooming pale pink in mid spring. It is deciduous but provides some winter interest by developing seed pods. Propagate by seed.

Allium senescens glaucum	flowering onion	Full sun	5

Native to China and grows throughout the summer and has lavender-pink flowers. They grow in ordinary garden soil.

Allysum saxatile	basket of gold		

See "Aurinia saxatile' below.

Amsonia 'Blue Ice'	Dwarf Bluestar	Full sun to partial shade	4-9

Dark blue flowers in late spring and early summer with dark green leaves turning yellow in fall. 12-15"tall and propagated by division after a few years if flowering starts to decline.

Anacyclus pyrethrum depressus	Mt. Atlas daisy	Full sun	6-8

Mat-forming green filigree-like foliage with white rayed flowers from June through August 1" tall.

Androsace sarmentosa	rock jasmine	Full sun to partial shade	3

Native to the highest mountain ranges in the Himalayas and West China. This is an evergreen alpine. The rosettes spread by runners into an open mat and bear clusters of small pink flowers. Should be able to take a bit of shade. Primulaceae family. Propagation by seed, but requires a period of cold stratification and could take up to two years to germinate. Also easy to propagate by division.

Anemone pulsatilla	Pasque flower	Sun to light shade	4-8

Native to central and northern Europe and likes moist soil. Propagate by seeds or division in spring. The plant is poisonous but is used medicinally. Purple to redish, bell-shaped flowers in spring (around Esater, hense the name "Pasque flower").

Anemonella thalictroides	rue anemone	Partial to full shade	4-8

Ranunculaceae family, native to eastern North America. Blooms April to May with white or pale pink blossoms. Grows in ordinary garden soil. Grows to 9" tall and becomes dormant in summer.

Antennaria dioca	pussy toes	Full sun	3-5

Pink-tipped flowerheads bloom from early summer to fall in full sun. 4-12" tall, a member of the aster family (Asteraceae) which used to be called the daisy family (Compositae). This plant is a mat-former and likes a dry, poor sandy soil, well suited for rock gardens. Propagate by division or seed. Clusters of pink flowers show above the low foliage.

Antennaria microphylla	littleleaf pussytoes	Full sun	3-7

Asteraceae family, native to most of the United States and Canada. White flowers to 1' tall in mid spring.

Aquilegia akitensis

See "Aquilegia flabellata" below

Aquilegia flabellata	fan columbine	Full sun to part shade	4-8

Ranunculaceae family, also known as *Aquilegia akitensis*. Blue-violet blossoms from late spring to mid summer. Attractive to bees, butterflies and birds. Do not overwater. Native to Japan, this is a dwarf form of columbine with one or two flowers per stem. They re-seed freely and colors vary depending upon the variety.

Aquilegia jonesii	blue limestone columbine or Jones' columbine	Part shade	3-6

Ranunculaceae (or buttercup) family, Native to U.S. A low, tufted perennial with numerous delicate leaves, usually with a whitish coating on the leaflets. Deep blue to purple flowers throughout the summer months. Grows to about 8" tall and cannot be successfully transplanted. Likes moist soil with limestone.

Arabis	rock cresses	Full sun	4

Cabbage family (Brassicaceae) which used to be called the mustard family (Cruciferae) and it is a very large genus. Flowers are small, vary from white to purple, blooming in the spring in full sun and a sandy soil. Propagate by division in spring or fall. Cut back after flowering for a fuller plant with solid new growth.

Arabis alpina	rock cress	Full sun to partial shade	3

Easy to grow in ordinary garden soil. Forms a low mat of rambling stems that produce white flowers in spring.

Arabis androsacea	rock cress	Full sun	6-9

Brassicaceae (cabbage family), 6-12" tall with white to pink fragrant blossoms in late winter to early spring and foliage is evergreen. Propagate by seed or stem cuttings.

Arabis blepharophylla	rock cress	Full sun to partial shade	3

North American native evergreen with pink flowers showing in late spring.

Arabis sturii	rock cress	Full sun to partial shade	4

Evergreen of unknown origin forming a low mat of shiny green leaves and white flowers on stems only 2 to 3" tall.

Arenaria montana	mountain sandwort	Full sun	4-5

Grows to 4" high with trailing leaves and flowers. A profusion of white star-like flowers bloom from spring to summer in ordinary garden soil. It is best propagated by seed.
Pink family (Caryophyllaceae). Cut back by 1/3 after flowering to promote new growth.

Armeria caespitosa	thrift or sea pink	Full sun	3

Native to Spain. Evergreen, with spherical pink flowers, similar to my *Armeria maritima*). Grow in ordinary garden soil with a neutral pH. This is the smallest *Armeria*.

| Artemisia | wormwoods | Full sun to partial shade | 3-7 |

Very large genus of the aster family (Asteraceae) which used to be called the daisy family(Compositae); Flowers are not showy and these plants are usually grown for their ornamental, silvery leaves. They do better in a poor, sandy soil than in rich soil. Esy to increase by root division or cuttings. Should be pruned occasionally to promote dense growth.

| Artemisia schmidtiana 'Silvermound' | wormwood | Full sun to partial shade | 3-7 |

Asteraceae family, spreading with a mounded habit in poor soil and drought. Native to Japan. Small herbaceous perennial to about 1' tall and should be cut back about halfway in July (before flowering). Propagate by division or stem cuttings. Foliage is silvery-green and dies back after frost. Yellow to white flowers are tiny, sparse to insignificant in August. This plant is also called 'Nana'and it is the only common Artemisia that has a prostrate growth habit and one of the few that is not invasive due to its rhizomes. Be careful with this one. It is very popular and in cool, dry weather it mounds into a silvery dome. However, in heat and summer humidity it flops down into a droopy mess.

| Asarum | | Shade | 4-6 |

Birthwort family (Aristolochiaceae); Woodland plants liking shade. Called wild ginger because of their strong scent and flavor. Good humus soil and plenty of moisture. Easy to increase by division of creeping rootstocks or by seed. The flowers are pollinated by slugs and are located near the ground and hidden by the dense foliage. I do not care for these plants in a rock garden because as they spread, to me, they look far better in a woodland setting.

| Asperula gussonii | woodruff | Full sun | 5-8 |

Rubiaceae (madder) family which is the same family containing coffee. Native to Sicily in Italy, to about 3" tall. Blooms are pinkish-white in May and June and the foliage is very cool with whorled, stick-like leaves.

| Aster alpinus | alpine aster | Full sun to partial shade | 2 |

Native to the European alps. This is a deciduous perennial with daisy-like flowers of various colors that bloom throughout the summer. Ordinary garden soil is fine.

| Aubrieta deltoidea | purple false rockcress | Full sun to partial shade | 4 |

Native to Southern Italy, Greece and Turkey. This is an evergreen with loads of purple flowers in spring, although other color varieties are available. They don't do well in extreme heat and need a bit of shelter from afternoon sun. They should be trimmed after blooming to promote full growth and good future flowering. Easily grown from cuttings or seeds.

| Aubrieta 'Royal Blue' | rock cress | Full sun to partial shade | 4-9 |

Forms a low cushion of evergreen leaves loaded with blue to violet flowers for several weeks in spring. Trim plants lightly immediately after blooming to thicken the plants. Ordinary garden soil is OK.

Botanical Name	Common Name	Light	Zone
Aurinia saxatillis 'Compacta'	basket of gold	Full sun to partial shade	4

Also known as "Allysum saxatile". Brassicaceae (mustard or cabbage family). Native to Europe and Turkey, this is an evergreen perennial that spreads readily with golden yellow flowers in spring. Ordinary garden soil is fine.

Bolax glebaria	plastic plant	Sun to partial shade	

Whorled, thin-leaf foliage, very interesting. (Apiaceae or carrot family, along with dill, fennel and parsley). Tiny yellow flowers in summer. Native to the Falkland Islands.

Callirhoe involucrata	Poppy Mallow	Full sun	4-9

Flowers are a wine-color and bloom all summer. Low-spreading stems, grows in ordinary garden soil and reseeds itself readily.

Campanula carpatica	tussock bell flower	Sun to Light Shade	4

6-12" tall from southern Europe with handsome blue flowers, although many white to sky blue varieties are available. This is a long-flowered plant which likes ordinary garden soil. Propagate by division, cuttings or seeds. Foliage is susceptible to slugs.

Campanula elatines garganica	bell flower or Carpathian harebell	Sun to Light Shade	5

Bell flower, somewhat sprawling, 6-10" tall. Blue, wheel-shaped flowers blooming early in the season with sporadic flowering until fall. They like ordinary garden soil and can be propagated by division, cuttings or seeds.

Campanula portenschlagiana	Dalmation bellflower	Full sun to partial shade	4-7

Mounds of purple bell-shaped flowers from late spring through summer, only 6-9" tall.

Carex fraserianus	Fraser's sedge	Partial shade	5-8

Native from Pennsylvania to Geogia and grows in rich mountain forests. It forms clumps of evergreen foliage and in late spring produces cone-shaped flower-heads with clusters of pure white flowers, a bit "exploded-looking" and fuzzy. Easy to grow.
(Also known as *Cymophyllus fraserianus*).

Celmisia	Alpine daisies	Full sun	7-9

Over 40 species, this plant is native to New Zealand. Flowers are typically daisy-like, mostly white and the leaves are sword-like and pointed, silvery and hairy.

Centranthus ruber	Jupiter's beard	Sun to partial shade	4-9

Easy to grow perennial with showy red flowers that should bloom all summer. Easily raised from seed.

Cerastium tomentosum	Snow in Summer	Full sun	

Pink family (Caryoophyllaceae) from Europe. Easy to grow in full sun and can be increased by division. Popular rock garden plant, 6" tall forming large patches. This plant tends to be invasive and persistent and will grow in pure sand. Be careful! Cut back after flowering for a fuller plant with solid new growth.

Chelidonium (SEE *Hypericum cerastoides* below)

Chionodoxa luciliae	glory of the snow	Full sun to part shade	3-8

A bulb in the Liliaceae family native to Turkey. Blooms from March to April with star-like lilac blue flowers and a white center to 9" tall. Bulbs should be planted 3" deep in ordinary garden soil. They spread forming a carpet of early spring bloom. Foliage fades shortly after blooming and the plants go dormant for the rest of the year.

Chrysanthemum weyrichii 'White Bomb'	Chrysanthemum	Full sun	4-9

Asteraceae family, growing 6-12" tall with pink to white blossoms in late summer to fall. Do not overwater. Propagate by division, stem cuttings or seed.

Chrysogonum virginianum	green-and-gold or goldenstar	Partial shade	5

Aster family (Asteraceae) which used to be called the daisy family (Compositae). 4-10" blooms yellow from spring to summer in moderately rich soil. Propagate by seeds or division. This is a North American native. Also known as *Dendranthema weyrichii*.

Claytonia virginica	spring beauty	Partial shade	3-8

Native perennial, about 3-6" tall. Flowers have 5 petals and 2 green sepals. They bloom white with fine pink stripes. Flowers open on warm sunny days and close during cloudy weather or at night. They bloom for a month in mid to late spring. It will reseed. The corms are edible and could be eaten by voles, etc. Member of the purslane family (Portulacaceae)

Cymophyllus fraserianus (See *Carex fraserianus* above).

Daphne cneotum	garland flower or rose daphne	Full sun to partial shade	5

Mezereum family (Thymelaeaceae) native to Europe and Asia. Spreading evergreen shrub to 12" tall with pink, fragrant flowers, blooming in spring. It likes ordinary garden soil with a bit of lime added. They do best in full sun but will tolerate partial shade. Trim off any winter "foliage burn" in early spring. Propagate from fresh seed or summer cuttings. Side shoots can also be rooted.

Delosperma	ice plants	Full sun to partial shade	5-7

These have succulent foliage, low spreading stems with many flowers of various colors from yellow to all shades of pink. Should be mulched with gravel to reduce heat and glare.

Delosperma cooperi	purple ice plant	Full sun	5-9

3" high foliage with daisy-like rosy-purple flowers blooming all summer long.

Delosperma floribundum 'Balosquin'	hardy iceplant sequins	Full sun	6-9

This is a new variety as of 2009. A groundcover with succulent foliage until frost. It blooms all summer with pink rays and a white center. Supposedly it is resistant to both heat and drought.

Dendranthema weyrichii

See *Chrysanthemum weyrichii* above.

Dianthus barbatus	Sweet William	Full sun	4-8

Carophyllaceae (pink) family, this is a biennial, 12-18" tall. Parts of the plant are poisonous if ingested. Blossoms vary from pink, red and white in mid summer with evergreen foliage. Do not overwater. Propagation is by seed. Even though it is a biennial, it acts as a perennial by reseeding itself. Ordinary garden soil is fine, especially if a bit on the alkaline side.

Dianthus deltoides	maiden pink	Full sun	3-9

Carophyllaceae (pink) family, perennial under 6" in height. Blooms in mid summer with pink to red to white blossoms with evergreen foliage. Propagate by division or seed. If the plant gets sheared after blooming, some flowers will continue throughout the season.

Dianthus plumarius	pinks	Full sun to light shade	3-9

Evergreen, from 12-18" tall, forming a mat of grasslike gray-green leaves. Fragrant flowers come in may and bloom to July in many shades of pink, rose, purple and white. Propagate by division.

Dianthus simulans	pinks	Full sun	5-8

This plant is under 6" tall with pink blossoms in late spring to early summer and evergreen.

Dicentra cucullaria	Dutchman's breeches	Part shade to shade	3-7

Native wildflower with fern like foliage blooming white from March to May. The plants go dormant in late spring to early summer. I have this plant in my woodland garden, not in my rock garden as I believe the plant more suitable in the woods.

Doronicum cordatum	Leopard's bane

Blooms in spring and summer with bright, yellow daisies.

Draba aizoides	yellow whitlow grass	Full sun	4-8

Brassicaceae family, growing under 6" tall. It blooms bright yellow in very early spring and has evergreen foliage. Propagation is by seed. Be careful not to overwater.

Draba lasiocarpa	Russian mustard	Full sun

Tiny plants from Arctic areas, a true alpine plant; Bright yellow & fragrant blossoms, usually showing through the snow in early March.

Draba sibirica	Siberian draba	Full sun	4-9

Brassicaceae family, this plant is native to Siberia and Greenland. It is a perennial groundcover blooming with yellow flowers.

Dracocephalum tanguticum	dragonhead	Full sun	5-9

Lamiaceae family, 6-12" tall, flowers are hooded, medium blue blooming from late spring to mid summer. The foliage dies back in winter and should not be overwatered. Propagation is by seed.

Dryas octopetala	Mountain avens	Full sun	1

This plant is 3" tall and spreads slowly with 6-10" tall seedheads and flowers. It is native to Washington state and blooms in spring and sometimes here and there throughout the summer. The flowers have 8 whitish petals and a bright yellow center. Dried seed heads are feathery, looking a bit like milkweed (*Asclepias*) and provide winter interest.

Edraianthus graminifolius	grassy bells	Full sun	4

Grassy foliage with prostrate stems and adorable violet-blue bells in ball-like clusters in June and July. Native to the Mediterranean to eastern Europe.

Epimedium x rubrum	red bisop's hat	Partial to full shade	5-9

Thrives in dry shade beneath trees, this is a groundcover that will spread, but not invasive. Heart-shaped foliage emerges in spring apple-green edged in red with crimson and yellow blossoms. Foliage turns all green in summer and then red in autumn.

Eranthis hyemalis	Winter Aconite	Full sun to partial shade	3-7

Ranunculaceae (buttercup) family, perennial under 6". All parts of the plant are poisonous if ingested including the seed. Blooms bright yellow in early spring. Needs consistently moist soil and cannot dry out. Probably not a great choice for a normal rock garden unless near a pond or bog. It can also be extremely aggressive, so be careful with it.

Erica carnea	Spring Heath	Full sun	5

Heath family (Ericaceae) from South America and the Mediterranean region. Small, needlelike leaves in dense clusters to 12" tall. Likes a not too rich acid soil. Prune hard in spring to remove tip injury and promote compact growth. Propagate from summer cuttings or by removing stems showing root development at the base. Long flowering period beginning in early spring with red flowers although other colored flower varieties have been developed.

Erigeron compositus		Full sun	5

North American native with gray foliage and daisy-like flowers in various colors from spring to early summer. Ordinary garden soil is fine in a dry location.

Erigeron glaucus	seaside daisy	Full sun	3-10

Asteraceae family, perennial, 6-12" tall. Daisy-like Blooms from pink to violet/lavender in spring with evergreen foliage. Drought tolerent so do not overwater.

Erinus alpinus	fairy foxglove or alpine liverwort	Full sun	4-7

Scrophulariaceae (snapdragon family) under 6" high, with pink, purple or white blossoms from late spring to mid summer. Evergreen foliage, and will reseed itself. Do not overwater.

Eriogonum umbellatum	sulfur flower or sulfer buckwheat	Full sun	3-9

Grows only 3" tall, it is a biennial native to west of the Rockies. Needs little to no water after it is established. Yellow flowers with gray foliage in late spring into summer. Average garden soil is fine, as is sandy soil. It will ressed and act as a perennial so don't cut back stems until seed has fallen to the ground.

Eryngium planum 'Jade Frost'	sea holly	Full sun to partial shade	5-9

Long leaves with bright pink edges and gray veins. Later on, the pink disappears, becoming white with 3" stems showing with tiny blue blooms. Very heat and drought tolerant.

Erysimum capitatum	coastal wallflower	Full sun	3-7

Perrenial in the Brassicaceae family, native to western North America. Grows to about 1' high with yellow-orange to copper-orange color from May to July.

Euphorbia characias 'Glacier Blue'		Full sun to partial shade	7-10

Beautiful variegated blue-gray leaves with creamy edges. Also, creamy-white flowers on 18" stems for several months. Plant maintains an upright habit without sprawling.

Euphorbia cyparissias	cypress spurge	Full sun	4-8

Herbaceous perennial in the Euphorbiaceae family, native to Europe. Grows to 1' tall with yellow flowers aging to red from April to June. Spreads by rhizomes and can be invasive so be careful. Also reseeds easily. Stems and leaves have a milky sap which can be poisonous

Euphorbia 'Helena's Blush'	spurge	Full sun to partial shade	4-11

Perennial to 12 or 18" tall with bright yellow blooms in late spring to early summer. It is actually grown for its foliage, like most of the Euphorbias. Do not overwater. This plant does not seed, as the flowers are sterile. It is evergreen.

Euphorbia myrsinites	myrtle spurge	Full sun	5-8

Native to Corsica, growing to about 6" tall. Blossoms are bright yellow from mid spring to early summer. Foliage is evergreen and blue-green. It is very drought tolerant and can be invasive so be careful. Propagation is by seed, but wear gloves when handling seed as plant can cause skin irritation. It is an invasive weed in parts of the western U.S. but seems under control in the east.

Euphorbia polychroma 'Bonfire'		Full sun to partial shade	5-9

Foliage emerges green in spring with bright yellow tips and then turn deep red for the entire summer.

Festuca ovina glauca	powder blue festuca	Full sun	5-8

Tuft-like grass clumps to 10" high of a unique blue foliage. Poor and dry soil is fine. It will multiply but it is easy to control. Highly ornamental.

Fritillaria meleagris	checkered lily	Full sun to partial Shade	4-8

Liliaceae family, a bulb, growing about 6-12" tall. Parts of the plant are poisonous if ingested. Blooms from white to pink to purple in early spring. Do not over water. Propagate by dividing rhizomes or from seed

Galanthus elwesii	greater snowdrop	Full sun to partial shade	4-8

Amaryllidaceae family, growing to about 1' in height by bulbs. They bloom white in early spring. The foliage is deciduous and disappears in winter. Propagate by dividing rhizomes or bulbs. Seeds can be collected by allowing pods to dry on plant and breaking them open.

Galanthus nivalis	snow drops	Full sun to partial shade	3-8

Amaryllidaceae family, growing by bulbs to about 1' in height. All parts are poisonous if eaten. Native to Europe, the nodding white flowers are usually the first of the early spring season. They do well in ordinary garden soil, the bulbs going dormant in summer. They do require constant moisture so don't let them dry out. Divide rhizomes and bulbs. Seed does not store well so sow as soon as possible. Score the base of the bulbs to promote new bulblets.

Galium odoratum	sweet woodruff	Shade	5

Madder family (Rubiaceae). Grows to 12" tall and tolerates shade. Tiny white flowers and likes a moist, slightly acid soil. In sunny, dry soil, plants become stunted and may die down. Easy to divide in spring.

Gentiana septemfida	gentian	Partial shade	3

Mountain native to Asia with beautiful blue flowers in late summer. Soil should be high in organic matter and they need to be shadede from direct, hot summer sun.

Geranium cinereum	hardy geranium or dwarf geranium	Full sun to partial shade	5

Native to the Pyrenees mountains between France and Spain. This is a bushy plant with gray-green leaves and pink flowers usually showing from spring to summer.

Geranium dalmaticum	hardy geranium	Full sun to partial shade	3

Native to Albania, this is a dwarf bushy plant with pale pink flowers.

Geranium sanguineum striatum	hardy geranium	Full sun to partial shade	3

Native to Britain, grows in ordinary garden soil and prefers partial shade. Grows about 1' tall with bright magenta blossoms.

Geranium wallichianum	Wallich geranium	Full sun	5-8

This is a trailing geranium, 6" tall with 1' long branches trailing over the rocks. Flowers are mauve and lavender blooming in late summer. The foliage dies back in winter. Propagation is by division or seed.

Geranium x cantabrigiense		Full sun to partial shade	4-8

Native to the Biokovo Mountains in Europe. Flowers from late spring to mid summer. The variety Biokovo' has white flowers with pink centers and 'Biokovo Karmina' has deep rose colored flowers. Will tolerate wet or dry conditions. Foliage is aromatic and turns red in fall. 6" tall.

Geum coccineum	scarlet avens	Full sun to partial shade	5-7

Rosaceae family, growing to 24". Blooms orange to red-orange in late spring through mid summer. Foliage is evergreen and can be propagated by dividing the rootball.

Globularia cordifolia	globe daisy	Full sun to partial shade	5

Native to Europe, a perennial forming a spreading mat of small leaves that roots as it spreads. Fuzzy rounded heads of pale lavender or blue flowers appear in summer. Ordinary garden soil is fine.

Gutierrezia sarothrae	broom snakeweed or perennial matchweed	Full sun	4-9

Native to western North America from central Canada to northern Mexico. Small dense, bushy shrub to about 1-1/2' tall. Plant flowers abundantly bright golden yellow. It is in the Asreraceae family. Plant is toxic to livestock

Gypsophila cerastiodes		Full sun	5-8

Native to the Himalayas, a low-growing perennial forming 2" tall mats that are semi-evergreen. Flowers are trumpet-shaped, colored white with light pink veins, with 5 petals in late spring. Doesn't like winter moisture and soil a bit alkaline is best.

Gypsophila repens 'Rosea'	creeping baby's breath	Full sun to partial shade	3-9

6" tall, blooming with pink flowers from spring to fall. Pink family (Caryophyllaceae). Soil should not be too rich. Propagate by seed or cuttings. Established plants do not transplant easily. Native to mountain areas of Europe.

Helianthemum nummularium	rock rose	Full sun	5-6

Native to Europe and North Africa.
Rock-rose family (Cistaceae). Yellow flowers resembling buttercups to 12" tall. Likes sandy, alkaline soil. Propagate by division or cuttings. Cut back after the first flowering to promote autumn bloom. Many varieties are available with a wide range of colors. Will tolerate dry conditions.

Herniaria glabra 'Sea Foam'		Full sun to partial shade	5-8

A new variety in 2009, each leaf of this groundhugger is edged with creamy-white. Very unusual lime-green, dense foliage.

Hepatica americana	liverleaf	Partial shade	3-8

Herbaceous perennial in the Ranunculaceae family, native to southeastern Canada and the southeastern United States. Grows 6-9" tall with blue, lavender or white flowers in March. Needs to be kept moist.

Houstonia coerulea	azure bluet	Partial shade	5-8

Delicate, low growing plant with pale blue flowers with a golden-yellow center

Houstonia serpyllifolia	creeping bluet	Partial shade	5-8

Native to North America, this is a groundcover with tiny evergreen leaves that are bright green and 2" long. Flowers occur in mid to late summer, tiny and violet blue to white. Keep relatively moist. This plant creates a nice moss-like effect which is very attractive in rock gardens.

Hutchinsia alpina		Sun to partial shade	5-7

Tufted perennial about 4" tall, native to European mountains. Pure white flowers bloom in late spring. Likes the soil a bit moist and a little on the alkaline side.

Hylomecon japonicum		Partial shade	5-8

Spring-blooming perennial from Japan with large golden-yellow blossoms to 1' tall in spring. Likes a woodland setting. Also known as *Chelidonium*.

Hypericum cerastoides	St.-John's-wort	Full sun	6

Native to Turkey, with bright yellow flowers showing in late summer and early fall. Creeping perennial, easy to grow and especially likes to crawl over rocks.

Ilex x 'Rock Garden'	rock garden holly	Full sun	6-9

Real holly leaves, dark green and very small. Forms a low, dense mound about 8" X 12" and needs plenty of moisture.

Ipheion uniflorum	spring starflowers	Full sun	5-9

Liliaceae family, bulbs grow to about 1' in height, blooming from white to pale blue in early spring. Do not overwater. Propagate by dividing rhizomes or by seed. Native to South America so it may need some winter mulch in the cold north.

Iris		Full sun	4

Iris family (Iridaceae). There are thousands of horticultural varieties. Stout rhizomes or bulbous rootstocks. Leaves are narrow, usually sword-shaped. Propagate species by seed and hybrids are easily divided.

Iris pumila	dwarf bearded Iris	Full sun to partial shade	2-8

Native to Europe and Turkey, a miniature of the well known bearded iris. Cultivars are available in practically every color to 6" tall. Easy to grow in ordinary garden soil.

Iris reticulata	Rock Garden Iris	Full sun to partial shade	5

Native to Turkey and Iran. These bulbs send up fragrant blue to purple flowers before the leaves appear and then go dormant in late spring. They will multiply and flower for years under normal conditions.

Isotoma fluviatilis	blue star creeper	Full sun to partial shade	5-10

Forms a dense carpeting of foliage topped with tiny star-like flowers from pale blue to white throughout the spring, summer and fall. A good choice to cover spring-blooming bulbs and also can stand up to foot traffic.

Jeffersonia diphylla	twinleaf	Partial to full shade	5-8

Berberidaceae family, herbaceous perennial to 6-12" tall. This plant is native to North America east of the Rocky Mountains. Flowers in very early spring for only a brief time with white, lovely flowers similar to bloodroot (*Sanguinaria canadensis*). Seeds are collected by ants as they ripen and sprout from nests in spring.

Knautia macedonia 'Mars Midget'	Pincushion plant	Full sun	5-8

Red flowers from June through August, 12-18" tall. Water well the first year, deadhead flowers immediately after flowering and cut back to the ground in fall.
Dipsacaceae (teasel) family, native to the Mediterranean and adjacent countries.

Lamium maculatum 'White Nancy'	Spotted Dead nettle	Shade	4

Height to 9", white flowers with showy silver leaves with green margins. 'White Nancy' is more restrained in spreading growth than other varieties.

Laurentia fluviatilis	blue star creeper	Full sun	5-9

Tiny star shaped flowers in May & June over a low carpet of foliage. Prefers some moisture, can be walked on and will stay evergreen in zones 8 and 9.

Lavandula stoechas	Spanish lavender	Full sun	6-9

Height to 2' with violet, lavender or purple blooms from late spring to summer. It is grown primarily for its silver-gray aromatic foliage and bees love the flowers. The variety 'Anouk' is only 10" tall, very compact and hardy in Zones 7-11.

Leontopodium alpinum	Edelweiss	Full sun	4-7

Asteraceae family, perennial to 12" tall, blooming from white to almost tan in mid spring. Propagate by division or seed. Originally from the Swiss Alps and is the Swiss national flower. Don't cut back dead foliage until spring as it is needed to protect the crown during cold winters.

Leucocrinum montanum	mountain lily or common starlily	Full sun	5-9

Liliaceae family, growing from southwestern North Dakota south to New Mexico, California and Oregon. This plant is a stemless perennial with grass-like leaves to about 6" tall. The flowers are fragrant, white with a slender tube about 4" long.

Linum capitatum	Flax	Full sun	6-8

Height a little over 1' blooming yellow in mid-summer with a mass of upward-facing funnel-shaped flowers. Native to southern Europe and easy to propagate by seed.

Lithodora diffusa 'White Star'		Full sun	6

Evergreen, narrow-leaved foliage with a slightly mounded form. Blossoms with a central white "star" with the petals outlined in vibrant blue in May and June. Grows 6-12".

Lychnis flos-jovis minor	dwarf flower-of-Jove	Full sun	4

Native to Europe, wooly gray leaves with pink flowers in spring. Will reseed itself.

Mazus pumilio	swamp mazus	Sun to full shade	6

Forms a carpet of green leaves with flowers resembling a lilac and white snapdragon in mid summer. Grows less than 6" tall and is native to New Zealand.

Mitchella repens	Partridge Berry	Shade	4

Grows to 2" tall, tolerates shade and is really happy in the woods in rich soil. Evergreen with white flowers and showy, scarlet berries. Native to North America, can be increased by division and is in the coffee or "madder" family (Rubiaceae).

Narcissus minor	dwarf daffodil	Sun to partial shade	5-9

Amaryllidaceae family growing less than 6" tall. Blooms in late winter or early spring with a bright yellow flower. Propagate by division.

Ophiopogon planiscapus 'Nigrescens'	Black mondo grass	Partial to full shade	6-10

Ruscaceae family, perennial to 6-12" tall blooming from white to lavender to violet in late spring and early summer. It is evergreen with almost black foliage. Propagate by division.

Orostachys spinosum		Partial sun	4

Very cool-looking plant, sometimes classified as a *Sedum*. Its rosette is looks like an artichoke with tiny leaves and spines at the tips. Native to Siberia. Propagate by removing and replanting offsets. The plant could flower after at least 5 years but the rosette dies after flowering producing offsets.

Papaver alpinum	alpine poppy	Full sun	4-8

Native to mountains in Europe, these have miniature flowers of white, pink, yellow and others 4" tall. They tend to naturalize themselves by reseeding and work well with other rock garden plants. Must be grown from seed as they are practically impossible to transplant. They will not tolerate wet feet and love a stone mulch.

Papaver rupifragum	Spanish poppy	Full sun	4-8

Papaveraceae family, this plant grows to 12-18" tall with a two-inch orange flower from mid summer to fall. The foliage is evergreen and is propagated by seed.

Penstemon

Native to British Columbia to Oregon and some from New Mexico and Mexico. Really tough rock garden plants. They are resistent to everything. Too much water, no water, too hot, too cold - they take it all! I have many. All sizes and all colors.

| Penstemon eatonii | firecracker penstemon | Full sun | 4-8 |

Scrophulariaceae (snapdragon) family, a perennial 18-24" tall blooming scarlet red in late spring and early summer. Evergreen, smooth-textured foliage. Propagate by stem cuttings or seed. This plant could be a bit invasive so be careful. Butterflies and hummingbirds love it.

| Penstemon 'Hidcote Pink' | beard tongue | Full sun to partial shade | 5 |

Salmon-pink flowers, evergreen that grows to 2' tall. Pinch plants after the first blooming and they will re-bloom. Cut back almost to ground before fresh growth begins in spring.

| Penstemon jamesii | snake-flowered penstemon | Full sun | 4-9 |

Also known as *Penstemon ophianthus*. Perennial, growing to about 12" with violet to lavender blooms in late spring and early summer with evergreen foliage. Propagate by division or seed.

| Penstemon menziesii | green mat penstemon | Full sun | 4-8 |

Very low-growing perennial with hugh blue to violet flowers in late spring. Evergreen with trailing stems that spread. Deadhead the flower spikes.

| Penstemon x mexicale 'Sunburst Amethyst' | Mexican beardtongue | Full sun | 5-8 |

Tubular purple flowers with white throats from June to September, flowering in the first year.

Penstemon ophianthus   See *Penstemon jamesii* above.

| Petrorhagia saxifraga (Was *Tunica saxifraga*) | tunic flower | Full sun | 4-7 |

Invaluable rock plant, flowering throughout the summer with small pink blossoms. Grows to 6" tall and spreads to about 1 ft. I grew it in my old garden as a perennial bed border plant and it was lovely - a bit like a low-growing gypsophila. Self-seeds prolifically.

| Phlox | | Full sun to partial shade | |

Phlox family (Polemoniaceae). About 60 species, mostly hardy and native to North America. Flowers are showy and varieties are available in many colors. Most like humus-enriched soil, except for *Phlox subulata* (see description below). Propagate from seeds, cuttings or division. Powdery mildew can be a problem in certain environments. Cut back after flowering to encorage new growth.

| Phlox douglasii | iceberg phlox | Full sun to partial shade | 5-7 |

Mounding, evergreen perennial with small dark leaves, producing small white, lavender-blue or pink flowers from late spring to early summer. 'Iceberg' cultivar bears white flowers, sometimes with a blue tint. Polemoniaceae (phlox) family.

| hlox subulata | Moss pink or ground pink | Full sun to partial shade | 3-9 |

Native to eastern United States. Evergreen creeper, tolerates dry soil, 6" high and forms a dense mat. Flowers are bright purple, pink or white with many colors in betweeen. Average garden soil is fine and not too rich (unlike most Phlox genera). For denser plants, shear stems back halfway after flowering usually mid to late spring; Also, cut back the entire diameter by half.

| Polygala chamaebuxus 'Kaminski' | | Full sun to partial shade | 6-9 |

Orchid-like blooms of pink and yellow in late spring and early summer, pleasant fragrance and evergreen foliage.

| Potentilla | cinquefoil | Full sun | 3-4 |

Rose family (Rosaceae). Yellow flowers from spring to summer on low-growing foliage. Propagate by dividing rootstocks in spring or fall or by sowing seeds in sandy soil. (Not sure about warmer locations)

| Potentilla alba | white cinquefoil | Full sun to partial shade | 5-7 |

Rosaceae family, about 6" tall with white blossoms in mid summer. Foliage is silver-gray. Propagate by division or seed.

| Potentilla aurea | golden cinquefoil | Full sun to partial shade | 5 |

Native to Europe, forms tight mats of deep green leaves and golden yellow flowers in spring. They like a rich, moist soil.

| Primula auricula | primrose | Partial sun | 3 |

Native to mountains of Europe. Usually, don't do well in full sun and found in woodland settings with moist soil.

| Primula denticulata | drumstick primrose | Sun to partial shade | |

Primulaceae family, growing 12-18" high with purple trumpet-shaped blossoms from mid spring to early summer. Foliage is deciduous and likes moist soil. Propagate by division and seed. Native to Afganistan and China. Flower heads are drum stick shaped, hence the common name.

| Primula frondosa | birds-eye primrose | Sun to partial shade | 4-8 |

Primulaceae family, this plant is less than 6" tall with a lilac-pink flower in late spring to early summer. The foliage is silvery-gray. Native to central Bulgaria where it grows near streams. Keep it moist.

Primula vulgaris	English primrose	Partial shade	5

The primrose family (Primulaceae) includes almost 30 genera with more than 800 species, usually perennial (or annual). Most are found in alpine regions but some occur in temperate zones; flowers on *Primula vulgaris* are usually yellow, blooming in spring but many colors and double-flowered forms exist. They like rich, moist soil and must be protected from direct sun. Sow seeds in spring or divide clumps every 3 to 4 years to improve flowering.

Pulsatilla vulgaris	pasque flower	Full sun to partial shade	4-8

Native to Europe, with early, tulip-shaped purple spring flowers. Established plants have deep roots and do not transplant well. Ordinary garden soil is fine. All parts are poisonous.

Puschkinia scilloides var libanotica	striped squill	Sun to partial shade	5-9

Grows to 6" tall with pale blue flowers with a thin deep blue stripe down the center of each of its 6 petals. Native to Turkey and surrounding areas (this particular variety from Lebanon, hence the name). Flowers during the month of April and goes dormant in the summer. The bulbs are very small and don't need to be planted too deeply (1-3" is fine).

Rosmarinus officinalis 'Irene'	creeping rosemary	Full sun	5-8

Creeping, spreading, hanging aromatic evergreen foliage with loads of tiny purple flowers.

Ruschia pulvinaris	shrubby ice plant	Full sun	6-10

Lovely foliage and showy flowers thriving in lean soil. They like it hot and dry. 3" tall, a cold hardy South African succulent native. Fuchsia-pink flowers bloom for 3-4 weeks in late spring.

Sagina subulata	pearlwort or Irish moss	Sun to partial shade	4

Pink family (Caryophyllaceae) related to "Arenaria", native to Europe.. 4" high and tolerates shade. (Sagina subulata 'Aurea' is Scotch moss & has golden-green leaves). Looks like moss but will not survive in damp shade like the true mosses. Propagate by division or seeds. Flowers are profuse and tiny, blooming white in summer.

Salvia officinalis	common sage	Sun to partial shade	5-9

Showy, deep lavender-blue flowers and dense, finely textured and scented leaves.

Sanguinaria canadensis	blood root	Partial shade	4-8

Early spring wildflower, 6-12" tall with a single white flower and yellow center. Propagate by division in fall-the reddish-orange root color is where the plant gets its name. Keep soil moist.

Saxifraga x macnabiana		Partial shade

Very tight, interesting looking large rosettes of dark green, white edged leaves. Flowers are white with red spots.

Saxifraga paniculata	rockfoil	Partial shade	2

Native to Europe, Asia and North America. Evergreens that are not easy to grow and require a cool climate but have beautiful masses of tiny flowers in many colors. They require bright light but not direct sun and suffer from draught. *Saxifraga paniculata* will form colonies and will spread through walls. They are easy to divide.

Saxifraga x urbium	London pride	Light shade	5

6" high with leaves light green in spring turning blue-green then dark. Pink flowers are not suited to hot, dry climates. Saxifrage family (Saxifragaceae). This plant likes "gritty soil" with lime. Propagate from seeds in early spring or division of rootstocks in spring or summer.

Scabiosa graminifolia 'Butterfly Blue'	grass-leaf scabious	Full sun	6

Native of Europe, this plant has long, narrow silvery leaves with lavender-blue flowers which bloom most of the summer. Ordinary garden soil is fine and they will reseed themselves.

Scilla siberica	Siberian squill	Part sun to part shade	3-8

Mature height of this bulb plant is about 8" tall with tiny, nodding, blue star-like flowers. Bulbs should be planted in fall, close together as they are small. Do not remove foliage until it is yellow. Remember, in the rock garden, once the foliage dies back in summer, the ground will be bare. Maybe some creeping thyme or similar spreader would work to cover the "sleeping" bulbs.

Scutellaria alpina	Alpine skullcap	Full sun to partial shade	5-9

Lamiaceae family, a perennial 6-12" tall. Blooms pale yellow to violet to lavender in mid summer until fall. Evergreen, silver-gray to blue-green foliage. Do not overwater. Bees and butterflies love the flowers. Propagate by division or seed. Native to Europe and Russia.

Scutellaria resinosa	prairie skullcap	Sun to partial shade	4-8

Long blooming with lavender-blue flowers through the summer, to 12" tall. Water regularly until the plant is established.

Sedum	stonecrop	Sun to partial shade	3-8

Stonecrop family (Crassulaceae). There are over 600 species of *Sedum*, mainly perennial, fleshy and found throughout the northern hemisphere. They have a very diverse habit, from creeping to upright. Leaves come in many varieties and flowers in many colors. They grow in ordinary garden soil and can be propagated by seeds, division of roots, cuttings or simply setting the leaves in a sandy soil.

Sedum hispanicum var. minus	Dwarf Spanish stonecrop	Full sun	2-9

Crassulaceae (stonecrop) family. Under 6" tall blooming pale pink in late spring to early summer. Normally grown for its foliage, velvet-fuzzy with good fall color. Propagate by division or seed.

| Sedum kamtschaticum | orange stonecrop | Sun to partial shade | 4 |

Erect perennial, 5-8" high with ovalish evergreen leaves and yellow, star-shaped flowers from late spring to early summer.

| Sedum lineare | carpet sedum | Full sun to partial shade | 5-10 |

Under 6" tall, this perennial blooms bright yellow from mid summer to fall. Evergreen silver-gray foliage, very drought-tolerant. Propagate by stem cuttings.

| Sedum sarmentosum | gold moss | Full sun to partial shade | 3-8 |

Crassulaceae family, perennial to 18" tall. Bright yellow blossoms in mid summer. Propagate by division, stem cuttings or layering. Easy to pull out if it spreads where you don't want it but be careful as it spreads pretty fast.

| Sedum seiboldii | October daphne | Full sun | 2-10 |

6-12" tall with rose to mauve blossoms in late summer to fall. Propagate from leaf or stem cuttings.

| Sedum spathulifolium 'Cape Blanco' | stonecrop | Full sun to light shade | 5-9 |

Native to the Pacific Northwest, perennial to 4" tall. Flowers in summer with star-shaped, yellow flowers in tight clusters. Ordinary garden soil ok. Propagate by short stem cuttings or division in spring. Rosettes are really pretty with green leaves covered with a silvery-white waxy powder.

| Sedum spurium | two-row stonecrop | Sun to partial shade | 3-4 |

This is a strong-growing creeper to 6" high; semi-evergreen with pink flowers in late summer. There are many varieties but be careful of it spreading too much!

| Sedum spurium 'Fulda Glow' | creeping red sedum | Full sun to partial shade | 3-9 |

3-4" tall semi-evergreen foliage with bright red, star-shaped flowers all summer to fall.

| Sedum ternatum | woodland stonecrop | Full sun to partial shade | 4-8 |

Crassulaceae family, this plant is less than 6" tall with white blossoms in mid-spring to early summer. Foliage is evergreen with a smooth, rubbery texture. Propagate by herbaceous stem cuttings. Don't overwater. This plant doesn't spread as much as many other sedums.

| Silene schafta | campion | Full sun | 4-8 |

Native to Caucasus, an alpine plant blooming in late summer to fall with rose-magenta flowers. Ordinary garden soil is fine for these easy to grow plants. Easy to propagate by division.

| Silene pennsylvanica | rock pink or catchfly | | 4-8 |

Native, dwarf plant forming dense patches of purplish-rose flowers from April to June. Propagate by seed.

| Silene virginica | fire pink | Full sun to part shade | 4-8 |

Herbaceous perennial in the Carophyllaceae (pink) family. Native to eastern North America. Grows to 1 or 1-1/2' tall and blooms red from June to August with star-like flowers.

| Sisyrinchium angustifolium | Stout blue-eyed grass | Sun to partial shade | 3-8 |

Iradaceae family, perennial, 12-18" tall. Bloom colors white to light blue in mid spring, but usually grown for its foliage. Propagate by division or seed. Plant looks like grass when not in bloom.

| Sisyrinchium bermudianum | blue-eyed grass | Full sun to partial shade | 6-9 |

Perennial with grassy foliage with a neat shape and masses of indigo-blue daisies from midsummer to early fall.

| Soldanella alpina rotundifolia. | alpine snow bells | Partial sun to partial shade | 5-7 |

It is in the primrose family (Primulaceae) and grows to 3" tall, native to the Swiss Alps. Pale blue dangling flowers bloom April through June and remind me of upside-down badminton "birdies".

| Solidago cutleri | goldenrod | Full sun | 4 |

Eastern North American mountain native, forming clumps of large leaves with tight clusters of bright yellow flowers on short stems. They do well in ordinary garden soil.

Teucrium chamaedrys
wall germander
Full sun   5-9

Broadleaf evergreen in the Lamiaceae family, native to Europe. Grows to 1' tall and blooms in May with rosy lavender to purple flowers. Pinch or shear stems after flowering to promote bushy, compact growth. Many need some winter protection in really cold winters.

| Thalictrum coreanum | meadow rue | Partial shade | 4 |

Native to northern Asia, this plant has clusters of spherical lavender-pink flowers blooming in spring. They require a richer, moist acid soil and shelter from direct sun. Most of the meadow rues are too tall for the rock garden.

| Thymus praecox articus | Mother of thyme | Full sun | 4 |

Native to Europe, a creeping shrub with tiny, aromatic leaves, forming a ground cover, with flowers of red, pink or white in summer. They do well in a hot, dry location and poor soil.

Thymus praecox 'Coccineus'	Mother of thyme	Full sun to partial shade	4-9

3" tall spreading mat of evergreen foliage and a mass of brilliant crimson flowers in June and July. I planted it in my last garden as a ground cover around blueberry bushes which was very effective.

Thymus pseudolanuginosus	Wooly thyme	Full sun	4

Mint family (Labiatae), growing to 1" tall and does well in dry soil. It is native to the Mediterranean region, has prostrate leaves with only a few tiny, pink flowers.

Thymus x citriodorus	Lemon or lime thyme	Full sun	5-8

Lamiaceae family, under 6" blooming pink from late spring into summer. Very attractive to bees and butterflies. Bright green leaf with a nice citrus aroma.

Tunica saxifrage (SEE *Petrorhagia saxifraga* above)

Valeriana arizonica	Arizona valerian	Full sun	3-8

This is a native plant to the western U.S. It has clusters of bright purple flowers and basal leaves, found in nature at upper elevations on moist, north facing hillsides. The flowers remind me of small, spring-blooming *Viburnum*. It is only 6-9" tall and the flowers are pink-ish in color. It grows from Alaska south, through Canada and the U.S., a very widespread plant.

Veronica	speedwell	Sun to partial shade	5

Snapdragon family (Scrophulariaceae). Over 250 species suitable for rock gardens. They all like average to rich soil. Generally, they are 4" tall and can be divided after flowering is finished. Some species can be grown from seeds and cultivars from cuttings.

Veronica 'Blue Reflections'	creeping speedwell	Full sun	4-9

Only 3" tall with profuse, true blue flowers starting in mid spring.

Veronica incana
woolly speedwell
Full sun
3-5

White, hairy herb to 15" tall and mat-forming. Flowers with blue spikes nearly 6" long in midsummer. Native to Russia. Ordinary garden soil is fine in a dry, open area.

Veronica pectinata	wooly veronica	Full sun to partial shade	4-9

Perennial under 6" tall, blooming blue repeatedly throughout the year. Foliage is evergreen, blue-green in color with velvet-like leaves. Propagate by division, cuttings or layering.

Veronica rupestris 'Heavenly Blue'	heavenly blue speedwell	Full sun to partial shade	4-9

4" tall spreading to 18". This plant is a vigorous prostrate grower with deep green shiny leaves and deep blue flowers.

Veronica 'Waterperry Blue'	speedwell	Full sun to partial shade	4-8

Perennial under 6" tall with blue to violet blooms from late spring through the summer. Do not overwater. Propagate only by divisions as plants are sterile and do not set seed (or they will not come true from seed).

Viola comuta 'Rebecca'		Full sun to full shade	5-8

Vanilla fragrance, white flowers with blue-violet borders to 10" tall, blooming May through October.

Viola labradorica	Labrador violet	Full sun to partial shade	5

Violet family (Violaceae). Over 500 species distributed throughout temperate regions, including violets and pansies. About 4" tall with heart-shaped leaves and purple flowers. They love rich, moist soil. A short-lived perennial maintained by self-seeding. They can also be increased by division and by separation of rooted runners. Violas hybridize readily in nature so confirming species is extremely difficult to impossible. American violets have little or no color and the European ones are seetly scented. According to Louise Beebe Wilder "They should be somewhere in every rock garden".

Vitaliana primuliflora	Vitaliana	Full sun	4

This is a genus all to itself, a member of the Primulaceae family which unfortunately has had many names assigned to it in the past. Native to the south of Spain through the Alps and south through the Apennine Mountains of Italy, it has been found growing in high elevations to 12,000 ft (a true alpine plant). Carpeting, mounding shape with yellow flowers reaching upward in very early spring. Propagate by cuttings or by division.

GLOSSARY

Acid soil: Soil with a pH value lower than 7.0.

Alkaline soil: Soil with a pH value higher than 7.0.

Alpine plant: A plant that grows above the tree line at high elevations. They are generally snow covered in winter, thrive in the cooler summer temperatures and have a relatively short growing season.

Annual: A plant that completes its life cycle in one season, including sprouting, flowering and producing seeds.

Bare root: A plant sold in a dormant state with no soil mass around the roots and no stems, leaves or flowers.

Berm: A mound or wall of earth.

Biennial: A plant whose life span extends to (2) growing seasons, sprouting in the first growing season and then flowering, producing seed and dying in the second year.

Bud: A young and undeveloped leaf, flower or shoot.

Bulb: A short, underground stem, the swollen portion consisting mainly of fleshy, food-storing scale leaves.

Cairn: A collection of stones piled up for use as a landmark or monument.

Compost: A mixture of decayed organic matter used for fertilizing and conditioning soil.

Creeping: Prostrate or trailing over the ground or over other plants.

Crown: That part of a plant between the roots and the stem, usually at soil level.

Cultivar: An unvarying plant variety while under cultivation, either designed or just by chance, having both unique characteristics and is capable of asexual propagation. Originally, it was called a "cultivated

	variety" and is written after the genus and species in non-italics print inside single quotation marks.
Cutting:	A piece of plant without roots that if set in a rooting medium can develop roots and be potted (or planted) as a new plant.
Deadheading:	Removing faded flowers from plants before the seed begins to ripen.
Deciduous:	A plant that looses its leaves in winter; Non evergreen.
Division:	Propagation of a plant by separating it into two or more pieces, each of which has at least one bud and some roots.
Dormancy:	A state that a plant has gone into, being temporarily inactive and at rest.
Edging:	Cutting a shallow, "V-shaped" ditch to serve as an edge or border to a garden bed.
Fertilizer:	Any material used to enrich the soil for growing and feeding plants.
Genus:	A group of plants closely related and very similar to one another, normally written in italics with the first letter capitalized; the first part of the scientific name of a species. Plural: "Genera".
Germinate:	To sprout (applied to seeds).
Harden off:	Allowing plants to adjust to outdoor weather conditions gradually, by placing them in an area protected from direct sun, wind and cool nights for a few days prior to transplanting directly into the garden environment.
Hardiness:	The ability of a plant living outdoors to survive harsh weather conditions such as a freezing winter.
Hardiness Zone:	The USDA divided the United States and southern Canada into 11 "zones" based on average minimum temperature. Each zone indicates whether a perennial plant can survive the winter.
Herbaceous:	A perennial plant that has no woody parts and tends to die back to the ground after the end of its growing season.

Horticulture:	The cultivation of plants for ornament or food.
Humus:	Dark organic matter in soil, produced by decomposition of vegetable or animal matter, essential to fertility and a favorable moisture supply.
Hybrid:	A cross (the offspring) between plants from two different genera, species, subspecies or clones and denoted by a multiplication sign after the genus name.
Hypertufa:	A porous, lightweight container, made out of a mixture of Portland cement, perlite and sphagnum moss resembling "tufa", a natural form of lightweight limestone.
Invasive:	Agressively spreading from the original site of planting.
Layering:	A method of propagation in which the stem is induced to send out roots by surrounding it with soil.
Loam:	A loose soil composed of clay, sand and organic matter in the right proportion for plant fertility and favorable moisture supply.
Moraine:	Similar to screes with stony soil but far below the surface there is flowing water that deep roots can penetrate and absorb (usually at the foot of a glacier with continuing melting ice.
Mulch:	Protective material placed on top of soil and around the base of plants to help conserve moisture, keep weeds down, look pleasing, cool the roots in summer and keep them warmer in winter.
Mycorrhizal:	The symbiotic relationship between a fungus and the roots of a plant.
Neutral soil:	Soil that is neither acid nor alkaline, having a pH value of 7.0.
Node:	The place on a stem where leaves or branches are attached.
Organic:	A substance derived from living organisms without the use of chemically formulated fertilizers, growth stimulants, antibiotics or pesticides.

Perennial:	A plant that does not complete its life cycle in one or two years but continues its life cycle for 3 or more years planted in the ground. An "herbaceous" perennial is a plant whose stems dies back to the ground level each fall and sends up new shoots and flowers for several successive years.
Pergola:	A structure consisting of parallel columns supporting open roof members of girders and cross rafters.
pH:	A symbol for the means of expressing the acidity or alkalinity of the soil where 7.0 is neutral on a scale of zero (acid) to 14 (alkaline).
Pollenizer	Plant that supplies the pollen.
Pollinator:	The agent (bee, moth, bird, human, wind) that transfers the pollen.
Propagate:	To produce new plants, either by vegetative means involving the rooting of pieces of a plant or by sowing seeds.
Prostrate:	Lying on the ground; creeping.
Pruning:	To cut off undesirable parts of a plant such as stems, roots, branches, etc.
Rhizome:	A horizontal stem at or just below the surface of the ground, distinguished from a root by the presence of nodes and often enlarged by food storage.
Rockery:	Rocks placed in the landscape in an arbitrary without design consideration or regard for any natural terrain. Plants can be equally as arbitrary.
Rock garden:	Utilizing plants grown in natural alpine or rock covered areas making use of surrounding stones that tend to mimic the plant's natural or wild environment.
Rock plant:	General term for any small or dwarf plant suitable for growth in a rock garden.
Saxatile plants:	Plants that grow in rock covered mountain areas, not necessarily above tree line or in alpine conditions.

Scree:	A deep accumulation of stone and gravel well drained and few nutrients usually found at the base of a rocky mountain cliff or open slope.
Seed:	A fertilized, ripened ovule, naked in conifers but covered with a protective coating and contained in a fruit on all other garden plants.
Species:	An individual plant's unique, common qualities or characteristics, normally written in italics all lower case; the second part of the scientific name of a species. Its members are potentially able to breed with each other and reproductively isolated from other populations.
Subspecies:	A naturally occurring geographical variant of a species.
Succulent:	A plant with thick, fleshy leaves or stems that contain abundant water-storage tissue. Cacti and stonecrop (Sedum) are examples.
Variegated:	Marked, striped or blotched with some color other than green.
Variety:	Written in italics, usually preceded by the abbreviation "var." (which is not italicized), representing a noticeable change in a plant that developed by chance but continues to produce offspring with the same "change". It is actually a category within a species that shows some difference to others in the species but not enough to warrant a complete change in species.

Vegetative propagation: Propagation by means other than seed.

Vermicompost: Compost created by the use of worms to decompose organic matter.

Vermiculite:	A volcanic mineral in granular form that has been expanded by heat to an extremely high temperature. It is completely sterilized. It is used to loosen heavy soils to allow maximum root development, improve drainage and allow for good aeration.
Weed:	A plant growing where it is not wanted, tending to overtake or choke out more desirable plants.
Xeric:	Water-saving gardens or plants used in dry regions with little rain, utilizing native plants, increasing organic matter in the soil, mulching and reducing lawn areas.

BIBLIOGRAPHY

American Nurseryman. *The Pronouncing dictionary of Plant Names*. Chicago, IL:
American Nurseryman Publishing Co.., 2006

Baumgardt, John Philip. How to Identify Flowering Plant Families. Portland, OR:
Timber Press, Inc., 2003

Bloom, Adrian. *Making the most of Conifers and Heathers*. Wisbech, England:
Burall Floraprint Ltd., 1989

Capon, Brian. Botany for Gardeners. Portland, OR: Timber Press, Inc., 2005

Cebenko, Jill J. and Martin, Deborah L. eds. *Insect Disease & Weed I.D. Guide*.
Emmaus, PA: Rodale, Inc., 2001

Cloyd, Raymond A., Nixon, Philip L. and Pataky, Nancy R. *IPM for Gardeners A Guide to Integrated Pest Management*. Portland, OR: Timber Press Inc., 2004

Cresson, Charles O. *Rock Gardening* (Burpee American gardening series).New York, NY: Prentice Hall, 1994

Cullina, William. *Native Ferns, Moss and Grasses: From emerald carpet to amber wave-serene and sensuous plants for the garden*. New York, NY: Houghton Mifflin, 2008

Cullina, William. *Wildflowers A Guide to Growing and Propogating Native Flowers of North America*. New York, NY: Houghton Mifflin, 2000

Ellis, Barbara W. and Fern Marshall Bradley, eds. *The Organic Gardener's Handbook of Natural Insect and Disease Control*. Emmaus, PA: Rodale Press, 1992

Farrer, Reginald. *The English Rock Garden*. London, England: T.C. & E. C. Jack, Ltd., 1930 (2 volumes)

Ferreri, Jack. *A Rock Garden Handbook For Beginners*. Millwood, NY: North American Rock Garden Society, 1999

Gillman, Jeff. *The Truth About Garden Remedies What Works, What Doesn't and Why*. Portland, OR: Timber Press, Inc. 2006

Grissell, Eric. *Insects and Gardens*. Portland, OR: Timber Press, Inc., 2001

Hamilton, Geoff. *Garden Stonework*. London, England: W. Foulsham & Co. LTD, 1991

Keane, Marc Peter. *The Art of Setting Stones & Other Writings from the Japanese Garden*. Berkeley, CA: Stone Bridge Press, 2002

Kingsbury, Noel. *Natural Gardening in Small Spaces*. Portland, OR: Timber Press, Inc., 2003

Kuepper, George, Thomas, Raeven & Earles, Richard. *Use of Baking Soda as a Fungicide*. Butte, MT: National Sustainable Agriculture Information Service (ATTRA), 2001

Lowenfels, Jeff & Lewis, Wayne. *Teaming with Microbes A Gardeners Guide to the Soil Food Web*. Portland, OR: Timber Press, Inc., 2006

Nardi, James B. *Life in the Soil A Guide for Naturalists and Gardeners*. Chicago, IL: The University of Chicago Press, 2007

Neal, Bill. Gardener's Latin. Chapel Hill, NC: Algonquin Books of Chapel Hill, 1992

Nelson, Lewis S. M.D., Shih, Richard D. M.D. and Balick, Michael J. Ph.D. Handbook of *Poisonous and Injurious Plants*. Bronx, NY: The New York Botanical Garden, 2007

Nichols, Beverly. *Down the Garden Path*. Portland, OR: Timber Press, Inc., 2005

Ogden, Scott. *Garden Bulbs for the South*. Portland, OR: Timber Press, Inc., 2008 (Revised from 1993)

Pavord, Anna. *The Naming of Names*. New York, NY: Bloomsbury Publishing., 2005

Perenyi, Eleanor. *Green Thoughts*.New York, NY: Random House, Inc., 1981

Perry, Dr. L. *Garden Flowers*. Burlington VT: University of Vermont, non-dated

Peterson, Roger Tory and McKenny, Margaret. *A Field Guide to Wildflowers*. Boston, MA: Houghton Mifflin Co., 1968

Pope, Nori and Sandra. *Color in the Garden*. San Francisco, CA: SOMA Books, 1998

Pratt, Mary. *Practical Science for Gardeners*. Portland, OR: Timber Press, Inc., 2005

Rhoads, Ann Fowler and Block, Timothy A. *The Plants of Pennsylvania*. Philadelphia, PA: University of Pennsylvania Press, 2000

Rodale, J.I. *The Encyclopedia of Organic Gardening*. Emmaus, PA: Rodale Books, Inc., 1971

Sanderson, Carol A. *A Guide to Common Pennsylvania Wildflowers*. Reedsville, PA: Breezewood Publications, 2006

Sorin, Fran. *Digging Deep*. New York, NY: Time Warner Book Group, 2004

Stein, Sara. *My Weeds A Gardener's Botany*. Gainesville, FL: University Press of Florida, 1988

Stein, Sara. *Noah's Garden Restoring the Ecology of Our Own Back Yards*. New York, NY: Houghton Mifflin Company, 1993

Stein, Sara. *Planting Noah's Garden Further Adventures in Backyard Ecology*. New York, NY: Houghton Mifflin Company, 1997

Stearn, William T. *Botanical Latin*. Portland, OR: Timber Press, Inc., 1966

Streep, Peg. *Spiritual Gardening creating sacred space outdoors*. Makawao, Maui, HI: Inner Ocean Publishing, Inc., 1999

Tallamy, Douglas W. *Bringing Nature Home*. Portland, OR: Timber Press, Inc., 2007

Thresh, J.M. "Cropping Practices and Virus Spread" in *Annual Review of Phytopathology* 1982, 20:193-218.

Uva, Richard H., Neal, Joseph C. and DiTomaso, Joseph M. *Weeds of the Northeast*. Ithaca, NY: Cornell University Press, 1997

Wann, David. *The Zen of Gardening in the High and Arid West*. Golden, CO: Fulcrum Publishing, 2003

Wilder, Louise Beebe. *Pleasures & Problems of a Rock Garden*. Point Roberts, WA: Hartley & Marks, Inc., 1998

Wilder, Louise Beebe. *The Rock Garden*. Garden City, NY: Doubleday, Doran & Co., Inc., 1935

Zvolanek, Zdenek. *The Crevice Garden and Its Plants*. Pershore, UK: Alpine Garden Society, 2008
www.alpinegardensociety.net

SOURCES

Albrecht's Garden Center
650 Montgomery Avenue
Narberth, PA 19072
610-664-4300
Many rock garden plants but no catalog and they don't ship

Alpine-L
The Electronic Rock Garden Society
www.thealpinegarden.com
Free source for rock garden information and photographs.

A.M. Leonard, Inc.
241 Fox Drive
Piqua, Ohio 45356-0816
800-543-8955
www.amleo.com
Garden tools, equipment, labels

Avant Gardens
710 High Hill Road
North Dartmouth, MA 02747
508-998-8819
www.avantgardensne.com
Online catalog only but many rare or hard to find plants

Backyard Gardener
www.backyardgardener.com
Many interesting articles and information concerning rock gardens.

Big Dipper Farm
26130 Green Valley Road
Black Diamond, WA 98010
360-886-8133
www.bigdipperfarm.com
Online catalog only but great plant source

Bluestone Perennials
7211 Middle Ridge Road
Madison, OH 44057
800-852-5243
www.bluestoneperennials.com

Bonide Products
Oriskany, NY 13424
315-736-8231
Source for many organic products

Bowman's Hill Wildflower Preserve
PO Box 685
New Hope, PA 18938-0685
215-862-2924
www.bhwp.org/seed_catalog/index.htm

Burgess Seed and Plant Company
905 Four Seasons Road
Bloomington, IL 61701
309-662-7761
www.eburgess.com

Charley's Greenhouse and Garden
17979 State Route 536
Mount Vernon, WA 98273-3269
www.charleysgreenhouse.com
800-322-4707
Garden tools, instruments and equipment

County State Extension Services
www.csrees.usda.gov (Click on "Local Extension Office")
To locate your local extension service

Dave's Garden Watchdog
www.gardenwatchdog.com
Free directory including customer reviews of quality, prices and service of over 6000 seed, nursery and garden companies.

Dirt Works
1195 Dog Team Road
New Haven, Vermont 05472
802-385-1064
Neptune's Harvest fish fertilizer and other organic garden products
www.dirtworks.net

Doyle Farm Nursery
158 Norris Road
Delta, PA 17314
717-862-3134
www.doylefarm.com

Source for rock garden plants.
Enchanter's Garden
Hinton, WV
304-466-3154
www.enchantersgarden.com

Four Seasons Nursery
1706 Morrissey Drive
Bloomington, IL 61704
309-834-7200
www.4seasonsnurseries.com

Gardener's Supply Company
128 Intervale Road
Burlington, VT 05401-2850
800-863-1700
www.gardeners.com
Tools, supplies, organic remedies, compost and indoor electric kitchen composter.

Garden Markers.Com
446 Westfield Road
Charlottesville, VA 22901
www.gardenmarkers.com
Professional arboretum plant labels

Gardens Alive
5100 Schenley Place
Lawrenceburg, IN 47025
513-354-1482
www.gardensalive.com
Excellent organic source and guide for insects, diseases and nutrient deficiencies

Gempler's
PO Box 44993
Madison, WI 53744-4993
800-382-8473
www.gemplers.com
Commercial grade garden tools and supplies.

Helena Chemical Company
225 Schilling Blvd., Suite 110
Collierville, TN 38017
901-537-7280

www.helenachemical.com
Source for "Armicarb"

High Country Gardens
2902 Rufina Street
Santa Fe, NM 87507-2929
800-925-9387
www.highcountrygardens.com
An excellent source of rock garden plants

International Compost Tea Council
www.intictc.org

Inter-State Nurseries
1800 E. Hamilton Road
Bloomington, IL 61704
309-663-6797
www.interstatenurseries.com

IPM Images
www.ipmimages.org
Great photos for positive insect identification.

Jackson & Perkins Company
2 Floral Avenue
Hodges, SC 29653-0001
800-292-4769
www.jacksonandperkins.com

Joy Creek Nursery
20300 NW Watson Road
Scappoose, OR 97056
503-543-7474
www.joycreek.com

Keep It Simple, Inc.
12323 180th Avenue NE
Redmond, WA 98052-2212
425-558-0990
www.simpli-tea.com
Compost tea brewers and composts

Laporte Avenue Nursery
1950 Laporte Avenue
Fort Collins, CO 80521

www.laporteavenuenursery.com
Over 350 species of rock garden plants

Lee Valley Tools
PO Box 1780
Ogdensburg, NY 13669
800-871-8158
www.leevalley.com
Mattocks and many fine gardening tools

National American Rock Garden Society
PO Box 67
Millwood, NY 10546
www.nargs.org

National American Rock Garden Society Book Service
4411 New Holland Road
Mohnton, PA 19540
610-775-9084

National Sustainable Agriculture Information Service
PO Box 3838
Butte, MT 59702
800-346-9140
www.attra.ncat.org
Many horticultural articles and papers for free

Nativo Plants & Seeds
PO Box 306
Westfield, WI 53964
800-476-9453
www.prairienursery.com

North Creek Nurseries, Inc.
388 North Creek Road
Landenberg, PA 19350
877-3267584
www.northcreeknurseries.com
Source of rock garden plants

Organic Pharmacy
P.O. Box 2291
Asheville, NC 28802
800-819-6742
www.organicpharmacy.org
Source for organic dishwashing liquid and other products

Our Water-Our World
www.ourwaterourworld.org
Click on "Finding Pesticide Alternatives" for updated list of less toxic products.

Park Seed Company
One Parkton Avenue
Greenwood, SC 29647-0001
800-845-3369
www.parkseed.com

Peaceful Valley Farm & Garden Supply
PO Box 2209
Grass Valley, CA 95945
888-784-1722
www.groworganic.com
Organic seed, tools, books & many organic products including a hand hoe/pick;
Source for "Kaligreen"; they offer a soil-testing service and a booklet "Understanding Your Soil Analysis Report" explaining the test results and offering organic amendment suggestions.

Pharm Solutions, Inc.
2023 E. Sims Way Suite 358
Port Townsend, WA 98368
info@pharmsolutionsinc.com
Organic horticultural oils and pesticides

Pinetree Garden Seeds
PO Box 300
New Gloucester, ME 04260
www.superseeds.com

Plant Delights Nursery
9241 Sauls Road
Raleigh, NC 27603
www.plantdelights.com
Specializing in unusual perennials; Catalog costs 10 stamps or a box of chocolates!

Plow & Hearth
PO Box 6000
7021 Wolftown-Hood Rd.
Madison, VA 22727-1600
800-627-1712
www.plowandhearth.com
Source for many garden supplies including "Flowtron Leaf Eater" for shredding leaves.

Pollinator Partnership
423 Washington Street 5th Floor
San Francisco, CA 94111-2339
415-362-1137
www.pollinator.org

Prairie Nursery
PO Box 306
Westfield, WI 53964
800-476-9453
www.prairienursery.com

Profile Products LLC
750 Lake Cook Rd. Suite 440
Buffalo Grove, IL 60089
800-508-8681
www.profileproducts.com
Source for "Turface" mulch

RareFind Nursey, Inc.
957 Patterson Road
Jackson, NJ 08527
732-833-0613
www.rarefindnursery.com
Source for rock garden plants

Rock Spray Nursery, Inc.
Box 693
Truro, MA 02666
508-349-6769
Heaths & Heathers & other dwarf ericaceous plants.

Roots & Rhizomes
PO Box 9
Randolph, WI 53956-0009
800-374-5035
www.rootsrhizomes.com
Source for rock garden plants.

Seed Savers Exchange
3094 North Winn Road
Decorah, IA 52101
563-382-5990
www.seedsavers.org
Heirloom seeds, planting directions & gardening books.

Sunlight Gardens, Inc.
174 Golden Lane
Andersonville, TN 37705
800-272-7396
www.sunlightgardens.com
Source for rock garden plants.

Telos Rare Bulbs
PO Box 1067
Ferndale, CA 95536
www.telosrarebulbs.com

Timber Press
The Haseltine Building
133 S.W. Second Avenue, Suite 450
Portland, Oregon 97204-3527
www.timberpress.com

Toadshade Wildflower Farm
53 Everittstown Rd.
Frenchtown, NJ 08825
908-996-7500
www.toadshade.com
Source for rock garden plants

van Bourgondien
PO Box 2000
Virginia Beach, VA 23450
800-622-9959
www.dutchbulbs.com

W.A. Cleary Chemical Company
1049 Corporate Rt. 27
Somerset, NJ 08875
800-524-1662
Source for "FirstStep"

W. Atlee Burpee & Co.
Warminster, PA 18974
800-888-1447
www.burpee.com

Wayside Gardens
1 Garden Lane
Hodges, SC 29695-0001
800-845-1124
www.waysidegardens.com

Weed Science Society of America
www.wssa.net
Great photos for positive weed identification

www.whateverworks.com
Source for "Rainforest Sprinkler"-excellent tool for watering.

White Flower Farm
PO Box 50
Litchfield, CT 06759-0050
800-503-9624
www.whiteflowerfarm.com

Woodlanders, Inc.
1128 Colleton Avenue
Aiken, SC 29801
803-648-7522
www.woodlanders.net
Source for rock garden plants.

INDEX

A
Achillea 3, 27, 51, 62, 64, 92, 126, 149, 164
    Moonshine 3
acid loving plants 1
Aconitum 'Blue Lagoon' 28, 127
Agassiz, Louis 90
Agastache 15, 27, 39, 64, 149
    Agastache 'Acapulco Salmon & Pink' 149
Agencies, private regulatory 136
Agricultural Marketing Service 136
air circulation 5, 48, 75, 155
alcohol 113
alfalfa meal 52
Alyssoides utriculata 88
Alyssum 37, 139, 149
    Alyssum montanum 'Mountain Gold' 80
Amaranthus tricolor var. salicifolius 126
Amsonia 133, 165
anaerobic 52
Anagallis arvensis 62
annual 29, 36, 62, 145, 160, 180
Anthemis tinctoria 'Susanna Mitchell' 3, 149
anthocyanins 113, 114
antibiotics 103, 135, 136, 188
aphids 25
Apiaceae 115, 168
Appalachian Piedmont 110
Aquilegia x caerulea 'Red Hobbit' 26, 70
Arabis 74
    Arabis caucasica 'Snowfix' 53, 115
architectural interest 2
Arctostaphylos coloradensis 3
Armeria maritima 'Pink Lusitanica' 3, 150
Armicarb 77, 199
Artemisia
    Artemisia 'Little Green' 88
    Artemisia assoana 88
    Artemisia versicolor 'Seafoam' 3
artwork 36
Asclepias tuberosa 28
Asia 7, 37, 164, 169, 173, 181, 183
Aspen, Colorado 100
Aubrieta heterosis 'Novalis Blue' 50, 150
Aurinia 74, 164, 168

azalea 1
B
bacteria.. 24, 52, 138
bait 48
baking soda 76
balance 24, 79, 90
banana, dwarf.. 22
Baptisia 133, 147
bee balm... 1
beer 48
bees 64, 90, 91, 92, 157, 165, 176, 184
beetles 48
Bergenia 'Bressingham Ruby' 3, 150
berm 1, 2, 24, 37
berries 2, 50, 153, 177
Biaelowia nuttallii 112, 150
Birds.. 7, 90, 106, 139, 165, 179
    hummingbirds 7, 155, 159, 162, 178
Black-eyed Susan.. 34
bloom time 5
bogs.. 7
bone meal... 52
borders 61, 146, 185
boulders.. 1, 2, 61, 79, 133, 134
Brassicaceae... 37, 115, 153, 166, 168, 170, 172
Brooklyn Botanic Garden 1
buds... 37, 38, 39, 51, 55, 62, 80, 149
bulbs... 26, 122, 144, 146, 173, 175, 176, 180, 181
bulking agents 52
butterflies 91, 106, 155, 156, 160, 165, 181, 184
C
Cairn 186
Calylophus serrulatus.. 38, 62, 64, 150
Campanula 15, 28, 53, 64, 93, 106, 151, 168
candytuft, dwarf.. 3
Carex.. 21, 122, 168, 169
Carey, Jenny... 122
carotene... 113, 114
Caryopteris x clandonensis 'Longwood Blue' 28, 66
catalogs 2, 5, 7, 16, 23, 94, 106, 112, 144, 149, 164
Celandine 34
Ceratostigma plumbaginoides 27, 105, 151
Certified Organic 136
Chamaecyparis
    Chamaecyparis obtuse 'Nana Gracilis' 103
    Chamaecyparis pisifera 88, 102, 151
    Chamaecyparis pisifera 'Tsukumo'... 110

chemicals 90, 135, 138
chickweed 26, 62
Chionanthus 133
chlorophyll..113, 114
Cholla.. 21
cicadas 92
clay 1, 26, 47, 156, 188
Clinopodium georgianum 112, 115, 116, 127, 151
Coffin, Marian C... 110
cold frames 123
color 2, 3, 7, 36, 50, 51, 53, 66, 77, 91, 92, 93, 105, 106, 111, 113, 115, 122, 126,
    139, 149, 151, 152, 155, 157, 167, 168, 172, 175, 180, 181, 184, 185, 190
columbine 149
compost... 1, 25, 26, 29, 48, 51, 52, 54, 62, 65, 92, 103, 104, 105, 106, 112, 127, 128,
    137, 138, 149, 198
Compost Tea... 199
conifers,dwarf.. 1
contrast.. 4
Cornell University 76, 194
Corydalis.. 74
Cotoneaster
    Cotoneaster (C. apiculatus) 122
    Cotoneaster horizontalis... 2
cotoneaster, rockr.. 2
cottonseed meal 52
county extension 7
crabgrass 1
Crassula argentea 126
Crassulaceae 126, 181, 182
crocus..26, 122, 146
crown 27, 28, 35, 38, 55, 64, 176
Cryptomeria japonica 'Tenzan'... 88
cultivar...37, 127, 144, 145, 149, 151, 154, 178
cultural requirements 5, 111
cuttings.... 54, 61, 62, 65, 149, 150, 151, 152, 156, 157, 166, 167, 168, 169, 171, 174,
    178, 181, 182, 184, 185
Cypress 103, 151
D
daffodils..34, 122, 146
Dana, Susan 34
deadheading 64, 93, 105
debris 1, 26, 76, 104, 112, 138
design... 1, 2, 1, 2, 36, 46, 64, 77, 78, 79, 88, 189
dew 123
dew point 123
Dianthus..2, 3, 28, 52, 53, 62, 74, 92, 93, 122, 152, 161, 170
    Dianthus gratianapolitanus..2, 152

Digitalis obscura 3, 38, 62, 152
dirt... 52
dishwashing detergent... 76
diversity 7, 88, 138
division 54, 55, 149, 150, 151, 152, 153, 154, 157, 165, 166, 167, 168, 169, 170, 173, 174, 176, 177, 178, 179, 180, 181, 182, 183, 184, 185
dogwood 105
drainage.. 24, 46, 63, 65, 75, 89, 110, 137, 149, 159, 164, 190
drawing, scale 5
dry tolerant plants 1
dumps.. 4

E
e.coli.. 52
ecosystem 7, 137
edger 17
edging 36, 152
elevations 7, 110, 124, 153, 184, 185, 186
environments.. 1, 7, 144, 178
Eryngium planum 'Jade Frost' 172
Euphorbia
    Euphorbia 'Myrsintes' 105
    Euphorbia x martini 3, 38, 75, 127, 152
Europe 7, 8, 37, 150, 153, 154, 156, 157, 164, 165, 168, 169, 171, 172, 173, 174, 175, 177, 179, 180, 181, 183
evening primrose... 154
Evergreens 181

F
fall color.. 105, 116, 151
feather meal.. 52
ferns 74, 146
fertilizer... 24, 25, 38, 49, 50, 65, 103, 122, 135, 136, 197
Festuca 21, 105, 152, 172
    Festuca 'Elijah's Blue' 105
flies 91
flowering habit.. 7
foliage 2, 1, 3, 4, 5, 7, 14, 15, 17, 21, 28, 35, 37, 38, 39, 50, 52, 53, 54, 64, 74, 75, 76, 79, 80, 88, 89, 93, 103, 105, 113, 115, 116, 124, 127, 139, 146, 149, 150, 151, 152, 153, 154, 155, 156, 158, 159, 160, 162, 164, 165, 166, 167, 168, 169, 170, 171, 172, 173, 174, 176, 177, 178, 179, 180, 181, 182, 183, 184
foliar feeding.. 25
Forsythia 29, 34
foxglove, narrow leaf 3, 38, 147, 152, 171
frogs 48
frost 35, 65, 106, 123, 124, 127, 128, 139, 167, 170
frozen 3, 4, 15
fruit trees 1, 48
fungal ingredients 52

fungicides..135, 136
fungus 76, 89, 188
G
Galanthus...26, 146, 173
garlic 76
garlic chives 34
Gaura 15, 35, 64, 92, 93, 105, 106, 116, 127, 152
   Guara lindheimeri 28
genetic engineering... 136
Genista lydia 53, 153
genus 166
Geranium 27, 35, 51, 53, 92, 153, 173, 174
Geranium sanguineum 127
germander, gray creeping 3
Globularia cordifolia nana 88
gneiss 110, 133
government 135
grafts 61
grape hyacinth... 92
grass... 15, 26, 27, 28, 34, 35, 36, 65, 75, 150, 154, 160, 170, 172, 176, 177, 181, 183
gravel 21, 61, 153, 157, 169, 190
ground cover 144, 145, 147, 150, 151, 162, 183, 184
ground frozen 3
growth habit 7, 167
growth stimulants..135, 188
growth, spring 5, 15, 21, 23
Gypsophila bungeana... 88
H
Halesia 133
Hamamelis 133
Harden off... 187
Hardiness Zone Map 63
harmony 78, 138
heartleaf 3
Hemerocallis 21, 147
Henry Foundation 133, 134
Henry, Mary Gibson 133
Hens and chicks 75
Herbaceous vegetation 4
herbicides..136, 138
Herniara 21
Hibiscus 34
honeysuckle 133
Huff Church, Pennsylvania 61
humidity, relative 123
humus..1, 52, 150, 164, 167, 178
Hymenoxys 4, 15, 28, 39, 53, 92, 93, 115, 153

Hymenoxys scaposa 28
hypertufa 46
I
Iberis 3, 37, 38, 122, 153, 164
   Iberis sempervirens 'Little Gem' 3, 153
ice 15, 124, 169, 180, 188
Ilex 50, 88, 133, 139, 153, 175
   Ilex crenata 'Dwarf Pagoda' 88
   Ilex x 'Rock Garden' 50, 153, 175
Impatiens pallida 34
Imperata 34
Independent Organic Inspectors Association 137
insects 7, 25, 48, 90, 91, 138, 139, 145, 198
   beneficial 7
   eggs 7, 91, 93
Internet 5, 92, 149, 164
Ionactis linariifolius 112, 115, 154, 161
Iris 21, 34, 122, 175, 176
J
Jade 126
Jewelweed 34
Juniperus chinensis 'Shimpaku' 88
K
Kaligreen 77
kelp 52, 65
kitchen garden 1
L
labels 21, 101, 102, 111, 151, 196, 198
lambs ear 1
Land 23
Lavandula 4, 28, 126, 154, 176
   Lavandula angustifolia 'Nana' 4, 154
lavender... 4, 15, 51, 52, 62, 64, 92, 115, 126, 127, 139, 155, 156, 157, 161, 162, 164, 171, 173, 174, 175, 176, 177, 178, 180, 181, 183
lavender, dwarf English 176
layering 55, 153, 182, 184
leafhoppers 25
leaves 1, 2, 3, 4, 15, 17, 21, 25, 26, 27, 28, 35, 38, 49, 50, 54, 62, 75, 76, 80, 93, 104, 105, 106, 112, 113, 114, 115, 116, 122, 124, 126, 127, 128, 137, 138, 139, 144, 146, 147, 148, 151, 152, 154, 156, 157, 165, 166, 167, 168, 170, 171, 172, 173, 174, 175, 176, 177, 178, 179, 180, 181, 182, 183, 184, 185, 186, 187, 188, 190, 202
Lennilea Farm 61
Liatris 133, 160
light 5, 28, 49, 50, 76, 113, 139, 153, 154, 155, 161, 165, 170, 174, 181, 182, 183
Lilies 34
lizards 48

loam 1, 156

M
Magnolia 133
mammals 7
manure 1, 52, 103, 137
Manzanita hybrid 52
Mazus reptans 'Albus' 2
microbe 52
microclimates 64
minerals 52, 65
mint 34, 145, 149, 157
moisture 5, 6, 15, 23, 25, 46, 47, 48, 51, 75, 89, 115, 123, 147, 164, 167, 173, 174, 175, 176, 188
Monarda didyma 'Coral Reef' 1
moss pink 74
Mt. Cuba Center 110, 150, 151, 154, 159
mugwort 1, 26
mulch .. 4, 15, 16, 21, 25, 27, 29, 48, 50, 51, 53, 54, 63, 65, 75, 89, 94, 101, 103, 112, 114, 124, 127, 135, 138, 145, 153, 157, 175, 177, 202
municipalities 4
mycorrhizal 52

N
name, scientific 187, 190
names, botanical 126
Nasturtium 37
National Organic Program 136
National Organic Standards Board 136
Native Americans 7
nature 2, 37, 55, 77, 78, 79, 88, 90, 110, 126, 184, 185
nectar 7, 91, 158
nematodes 24
Neptune's Harvest 65
New York Botanical Garden 14, 193
New York City 1, 14, 88
nitrogen 25

O
October daphne 106
Oenethera 'Blushing Rosie' 1
oil, horticultural 76
OMRI 65, 77, 136
Opuntia 21
Oregano, ornamental 145
organic 1, 24, 48, 51, 65, 77, 90, 103, 104, 135, 136, 137, 138, 139, 145, 151, 155, 173, 186, 188, 190, 197, 198, 201
Organic Consumers' Association 137
Organic Foods Production Act 136
Organic Materials Review Institute 65, 77, 136

Origanum 'Rotkugel' 3, 92, 127, 154
oxygenation.. 52
P
parasites 76, 139
pathogens 52, 112, 113
paths.. 1, 138
Pelargonium endlicherianum 3, 154
Penn State 21
Penstemon.. 133
    Penstemon 'Blue Midnight' 3, 15, 53, 92
    Penstemon 'Mystica'..3, 62, 65, 66, 127
    Penstemon pinifolius 'Nearly Red' 3, 54, 155
    Penstemon x mexicale 'Red Rocks' 3, 62, 93
Peonies... 34
perennial 1, 25, 36, 48, 65, 66, 78, 79, 94, 105, 111, 144, 145, 146, 150, 151, 152, 153, 154, 155, 156, 160, 164, 166, 167, 168, 169, 170, 171, 172, 174, 175, 176, 177, 178, 180, 181, 182, 183, 185, 187, 189
Pergola 189
pesticides... 135, 136, 137, 138, 188, 201
pH 137
Phlox 29, 52, 55, 155, 162, 178
    Phlox paniculata 'David'..1
    Phlox subulata 1, 29, 38, 55, 62, 155, 162, 178, 179
Piatt, Vic 110
Picea abies 'Little Gem'... 4
pick mattock... 17, 29
pineleaf beardtongue... 3
pines.. 61
plants
    acid loving... 1
    alien... 6
    alpine..1, 8, 22, 24, 46, 61, 88, 122, 123
    aquatic 1
    bare root plants.. 5
    collector... 77
    cultivars.. 111
    disease.. 24, 75, 76, 89, 112, 150
    diversity... 138
    dormancy... 3, 17, 23, 26, 94, 106, 124, 128, 139
    dry tolerant.. 1
    dwarf.. 1
    growth 5
    heaved 26
    media... 48
    native.. 6, 7, 37, 61, 64, 91, 110, 111, 133, 134, 145, 146, 150, 151, 153, 154, 155, 158, 165, 166, 168, 169, 170, 171, 172, 173, 175, 176, 177, 178, 180, 183, 184, 190

North American 106, 145, 154, 155, 164, 166, 169, 171, 183, 192
nutrients 24, 65, 103, 190
planting 106, 143, 194
potted 5, 6, 187
rock 1, 2, 5, 1, 2, 4, 5, 7, 8, 14, 15, 16, 17, 18, 21, 23, 24, 25, 26, 27, 28, 29, 34, 36, 37, 38, 46, 47, 48, 50, 51, 52, 53, 55, 61, 62, 63, 64, 65, 74, 75, 76, 77, 78, 79, 88, 89, 90, 91, 93, 94, 100, 101, 102, 103, 105, 106, 110, 111, 112, 113, 114, 115, 116, 122, 123, 124, 127, 128, 133, 134, 139, 144, 145, 146, 147, 148, 149, 151, 152, 153, 156, 159, 160, 164, 165, 166, 167, 169, 170, 171, 174, 175, 177, 178, 181, 183, 184, 185, 189, 196, 198, 199, 200, 202, 203, 204
roots 16, 17, 24, 26, 38, 46, 49, 52, 54, 55, 66, 93, 94, 124, 138, 164, 174, 180, 181, 186, 187, 188, 189
seedlings.. 6, 17, 37, 48, 49, 50, 61, 124
shade loving 1
shipping.. 5
shock 6
spread. 2, 5, 37, 55, 63, 75, 76, 80, 92, 93, 102, 103, 106, 122, 127, 144, 145, 146, 147, 151, 153, 155, 158, 161, 165, 167, 169, 171, 178, 181, 182
subspecies 126, 188
varieties . 61, 112, 126, 139, 144, 150, 167, 168, 171, 174, 175, 176, 178, 181, 182
watering .. 6, 25, 35, 38, 50, 52, 53, 54, 55, 66, 76, 80, 89, 134, 151, 154, 156, 204
plumbago 92
poison ivy 133
Pollinator Partnership 202
pollinators 90, 91, 106, 138
pond 144
potager 1
Potentilla alchemilloides.. 88
powdery mildew 112
primrose...1, 179, 180, 183
Primulaceae 62, 165, 179, 180, 183, 185
propagation 48, 54, 127, 186, 188, 190
pruners 1
pruning..26, 29, 62, 112, 122, 128, 134, 138, 155
Prunus
    Prunus pumila 88
    Prunus subhirtella 'Pendula' 1
Q
quarry.. 4
R
rabbit... 38
rain.. 38
recycled materials 4
remedy 76
Rhododendron 133
rhododenron 76
roadside.. 4

rockcress 4
rocks 1, 2, 1, 2, 4, 5, 34, 36, 47, 61, 77, 79, 110, 112, 122, 139, 146, 164, 173, 175
   pulverized rock 52
Rodale, J.I. 194
Rodale, Maria 135
rooting hormones 54
rose 74
Rutgers University 153

S

Sagina subulata 1, 180
Salix 126
salmonella 52
Salvia 74, 126, 155, 180
sand 24, 25, 52, 61, 156, 169, 188
Saponaria
   Saponaria ocymoides 3, 156
   Saponaria pumila 88
   Saponaria x olivana 88
sawdust 52, 104, 137
Saxifraga arendsii 'Purple Robe' 17, 156
scale 1, 36, 65, 66, 77, 79, 106, 146, 186, 189
Scarlet pimpernel 62
Scilla 26, 146, 181
scissors 26, 62, 64, 114
Scotch moss 180
scree 1, 21, 110, 122, 159
Sculpture 36
Sears, Thomas W. 110
seaweed 104
sedge 65
Sedum 2, 3, 21, 27, 38, 50, 61, 64, 80, 92, 93, 115, 116, 125, 126, 139, 156, 157, 162,
   177, 181, 182, 190
   Sedum anglicum 126
   Sedum brevifolium 126
   Sedum cauticola 126
   Sedum cyaneum 2
   Sedum dasphyllum 'Major' 3
   Sedum hispanicum 61, 156, 181
   Sedum reflexum 80, 126, 139, 156
   Sedum rupestre 'Angelina' 38
   Sedum sexangulare 50, 64, 156
   Sedum spurium 'Dragon's Blood' 50, 64, 92, 93, 156
   Sedum spurium 'John Creech' 80, 157
   Sedum spurium 'Tricolor' 80, 157
seed ... 27, 48, 49, 61, 62, 124, 134, 149, 150, 153, 164, 165, 166, 167, 168, 169, 170,
   171, 172, 173, 174, 175, 176, 177, 178, 179, 181, 183, 185, 186, 187, 190, 197,
   201

seedpods 1
Seit, Robert 61, 75, 156, 157
Sempervivum 4, 21, 61, 65, 74, 126, 157
    Sempervivum tectorum 126
shrubs, woody 1
    azalea 1
    dwarf spruce 1
    juniper 1
    rhododendrons 1, 61
    Viburnum 133, 184
    yews 1
Silene 61, 75, 88, 157, 161, 182, 183
    Silene alpestris 88
slugs 48, 150, 156, 167, 168
snails 48
snow 1, 2, 15, 23, 26, 29, 139, 144, 169, 170, 173, 183, 186
snowdrops 127
Snowmass Mountain 100
soil 1, 2, 6, 16, 17, 23, 24, 25, 26, 28, 29, 36, 38, 46, 48, 49, 50, 51, 54, 55, 61, 63, 65,
    75, 90, 93, 101, 103, 104, 106, 115, 126, 135, 137, 138, 146, 149, 150, 151, 152,
    153, 154, 155, 156, 157, 159, 162, 164, 165, 166, 167, 168, 169, 170, 171, 172,
    173, 174, 175, 177, 178, 179, 180, 181, 182, 183, 184, 185, 186, 187, 188, 189,
    190, 201
    aeration 24, 52, 190
    amendments 23, 24
    knife 1, 16, 17, 26
    pH 23, 24, 114, 166, 186, 188, 189
    test 17, 23, 24, 201
    test-plugging tool 17
    workable 26
soy meal 52
species 21, 28, 37, 49, 64, 65, 90, 91, 93, 110, 111, 112, 122, 125, 126, 133, 145, 150,
    152, 153, 155, 157, 164, 168, 175, 178, 180, 181, 184, 185, 187, 188, 190, 200
speedwell 158
spiders 90
spores 76
spread 55
spurge, Martin's 3
Stachys byzantina 34, 80
stone 3, 4, 6, 15, 16, 24, 25, 27, 29, 34, 48, 50, 51, 53, 54, 61, 65, 74, 75, 88, 94, 105,
    110, 114, 122, 127, 133, 135, 164, 177, 190
stonecrop 34
    stonecrop, yellow 34
straw 26, 28, 137
strawberry 1, 26, 122, 127
Styrax 133
sulfate of potash-magnesia 52

sulfur 76
sun. 1, 6, 15, 18, 21, 35, 46, 51, 61, 64, 76, 78, 89, 103, 113, 122, 149, 150, 151, 152, 153, 154, 155, 156, 157, 158, 159, 160, 161, 162, 163, 164, 165, 166, 167, 168, 169, 170, 171, 172, 173, 174, 175, 176, 177, 178, 179, 180, 181, 182, 183, 184, 185, 187

T

temperature 15, 26, 29, 48, 63, 64, 89, 112, 114, 123, 137, 187, 190
Temple University 122
Teucrium aroanium 3, 157
texture 3, 182
thinning 49, 64
thyme 1, 37, 114, 126, 157, 183, 184
    thyme, caraway 1
    thyme, creeping see " 3, 38, 181
Thymus 1, 3, 37, 64, 88, 114, 122, 126, 157, 183, 184
    Thymus 'Ruby Glow' 37, 64
    Thymus herba-barona 1
    Thymus praecox minor 88
    Thymus serpyllum 3, 64, 114, 157
    Thymus x citriodorus 1, 184
Tilger, Mary 46
toads 48
Township 4
Trade Organizations 136
Tradescantia 133, 147
transfer stations 4
traps 48
trash 4, 26, 112
Treadway, Susan 133
trees
    cherry tree 1, 78, 105
    Cornus 61
    fir 1
    juniper 34
    locust 88
    maple 1, 113
    oak 113
    pawpaws 61
    pines 1
    redbud 61
    redwood 61
    Spruce 80
    viburnum 133
Trillium 133
tropical 1
trough 46
trowel 112

turf grass 36
Turface 21, 47, 202
U
Ulmus parvifolia 'Hokkaido' 88
United States Department of Agriculture 63
unity 79
University of Pennsylvania 74, 194
USDA Agricultural Marketing Service 136
USDA Certified Organic 136
V
Verbena peruviana 'Red Devil' 28
vermicompost 52
vermiculite 190
Viburnum 158
vinca 74
violets 185
virus 194
W
Wasps 91
Wave Hill 88, 102
weather, cold 4, 18, 154
weed 1, 6, 16, 17, 36, 62, 76, 102, 144, 145, 172, 204
wild strawberry 1
wildlife 7
willow 126
wind 6, 36, 78, 123, 187, 189
winter interest 2, 26, 135, 171
wood chips 52
woods 4, 46, 147, 170, 177
X
xeric 2, 35, 154, 155
Y
yarror, moonshine 152
yellow nut sedge 1
yew 1
Yucca 133
Z
zone 149, 164
    zone hardiness 2, 5

Photographs

Figure 1 Berm after weeding and mulching before installation of rock garden. 4
Figure 2 Rock garden in January. 15
Figure 3 Euphorbia x martini in January 16
Figure 4 Penstemon 'Red Rocks' in January. 17
Figure 5 Penstemon "Mystica" in January. 17
Figure 6 Lavandula Augustifolia 'Nana' in January. 18
Figure 7 Boulders at Brooklyn Botanic Garden in January. 19
Figure 8 Rock Garden at Brooklyn Botanic Garden in January 19
Figure 9 Rock Garden in Early February. 25
Figure 10 Rock Garden in February. 26
Figure 11 The rock garden at Penn State in March. 36
Figure 12 Close up view of Penn State's rock garden in March 37
Figure 13 Rock garden in March after "Spring Cleaning". 38
Figure 14 Freshly planted Phlox subulata 'Blue Emerald' in March. 39
Figure 15 April in Susan Dana's rock garden. 46
Figure 16 Susan Dana's rock garden. 47
Figure 17 Sculpture installed. 48
Figure 18 Permanent labels. 49
Figure 19 April view of rock garden from deck. 50
Figure 20 Rock garden in April after pruning. 51
Figure 21 Mary Tilger's rock garden. 62
Figure 22 Genista in May. 63
Figure 23 Geranium in May. 64
Figure 24 Saponaria in May. 65
Figure 25 Armeria in May. 66
Figure 26 Robert Seit's Alpine plants. 73
Figure 27 Robert Seit's Rock garden. 74
Figure 28 Anthemis tinctoria 'Susanna Mitchell'. 75
Figure 29 Aquilegia x caerulea 'Red Hobbit'. 76
Figure 30 Calylophus serrulatus with lavender. 77
Figure 31 Geranium sanguineum 'Max Frei'. 78
Figure 32 Rock garden in June. 79
Figure 33 Right rock wall at Morris Arboretum. 87
Figure 34 Left rock wall at Morris Arboretum. 88
Figure 35 Close up of rock wall at Morris Arboretum. 89
Figure 36 July rock garden. 90
Figure 37 Sempervivum 'Red Beauty' in flower. 91
Figure 38 Sempervivum dual flowers. 92
Figure 39 West rock garden in July. 93
Figure 40 Sedum reflexum 'Blue Spruce' in August. 101
Figure 41 Ceratostigma plumbaginoides (plumbago) in August. 102
Figure 42 Wave Hill rock garden (left). 103
Figure 43 Wave Hill rock garden (center). 104

Figure 44 Wave Hill rock garden (right side). 105
Figure 45 Chamaecyparis obtuse 'Nana Gracilis'. 113
Figure 46 Rock garden in September. 114
Figure 47 Chamaecyparis pisifera 'Tsukumo'. 115
Figure 48 Vic Piatt at Mt. Cuba rock garden. 123
Figure 49 Mt. Cuba scree garden. 124
Figure 50 Clinopodium georgianum. 125
Figure 51 Sedum Sieboldii (October daphne). 126
Figure 52 New rocks installed in October. 127
Figure 53 Temple Ambler's rock garden. 135
Figure 54 Temple Ambler's rock garden close-up. 136
Figure 55 November rock garden close-up. 137
Figure 56 November rock garden. 138
Figure 57 December rock garden. 146
Figure 58 Henry Foundation lower rock garden. 146
Figure 59 Henry Foundation upper rock garden. 147

BIOGRAPHY

Ron Kushner was trained formally as an architect at Drexel University prior to attending the 3-year Horticulture Program of The Barnes Foundation in Merion, Pennsylvania.

He is a Master Gardener and PA. Certified Horticulturist, currently employed by Albrecht's Nursery and Garden Center in Narberth, PA.

His organic internship was served at Worden Farm in Punta Gorda, Florida.

Aside from the continual evolution of his own half-acre garden, he has been involved for many years in the design, construction and maintenance of many gardens throughout the Philadelphia area.

Made in the USA
Charleston, SC
03 March 2010